THE BIRTH OF A KINGDOM

Studies in I-II Samuel and
I Kings 1-11

THE BIRTH OF A KINGDOM

Studies in I-II Samuel and I Kings 1-11

by

John J. Davis

BAKER BOOK HOUSE
Grand Rapids, Michigan

Library of Congress Catalog Card Number: 79-129927

Copyright 1970 by Brethren Missionary Herald

Baker Book House Company and BMH Books — copublishers

ISBN: 0-8010-2803-5

First printing, August 1970
Second printing, January 1972
Third printing, February 1974

PRINTED IN THE UNITED STATES OF AMERICA

To
My Parents
in thanksgiving for a
Christian home and a godly example.

ACKNOWLEDGMENTS

The author wishes to express special appreciation to the following individuals who made valuable contributions to the preparation and production of this volume:

My wife Carolyn and Mrs. Irene Anderson who typed the manuscripts.

Dr. John C. Whitcomb who made many helpful suggestions regarding the content and style of this volume.

Mr. Robert Ibach who prepared the chronological chart and maps.

Dr. S. Herbert Bess who prepared the Foreword and made helpful suggestions on the style and content of the manuscript.

Dr. Benjamin Hamilton who graciously prepared the index to this volume.

Mr. Benjamin Tollison for checking Biblical references.

CONTENTS

LIST OF ILLUSTRATIONS

Photo Credits

The Matson Photo Service, Alhambra, California 91803
Levant Photo Service, Box 89, Glen Ellyn, Illinois 60137
The Oriental Institute, University of Chicago,
   1155 East 58th Street, Chicago, Illinois 60637
Tekoa Archaeological Expedition

TRANSLITERATION

Whenever possible, Hebrew and Greek words have been transliterated according to the following form:

Greek	Consonants	Vocalization
α — a	א — '	— ā
ᾳ — a	ב — b, b̲	— a
ε — e	ג — g, g̲	— e
η — ē	ד — d, d̲	— ē
o — o	ה — h	— ê
ω — ō	ו — w	— i
ζ — z	ז — z	— î
	ח — ḥ	
θ — th	ט — ṭ	— o
ξ — x	י — y	— û
υ — u	כ — k, k̲	— u
φ — ph	ל — l	— ( )e
χ — ch	מ — m	
ψ — ps	נ — n	— ( )a
' — h	ס — s	
	ע — '	
	פ — p, p̲	
	צ — ṣ	
	ק — q	
	ר — r	
	שׂ — ś	
	שׁ — š	
	ת — t, t̲	

PREFACE

Priests, prophets, outlaws, giants and kings are all part of the exciting story of the kingdom period in ancient Israel. The captivating history of this important era in Israel's history includes major military conflicts, family feuds and spiritual failure and success. The historiographical methodology of the writers of the books of Samuel and Kings is quite unique in its approach to the monarchy. Official historians of that period, especially in Egypt, had a tendency to color royal history so as always to present the king in a favorable light. Seldom does one read about the military, political and spiritual failures of a king.

Of special interest in the books of Samuel is the constant personal touch of the historian under the inspiration of the Holy Spirit. The friends and members of the king's family are an integral part of the narratives.

This volume is primarily concerned with the text of the books of Samuel and I Kings 1—11 which record the rise and development of the united monarchy in Israel. Where appropriate, reference is made to the Hebrew text, ancient Near Eastern history and archaeology. Since space did not permit extended Biblical quotations, the reader is encouraged to have a Bible near when reading this volume. The documentation provided should help the reader in studying certain problems in greater depth. It is the author's desire that this volume not only be informative and intellectually stimulating, but also of significant practical value in Christian living and growth.

FOREWORD

S. Herbert Bess, Ph.D.

It is a pleasure to commend to the public the work of my colleague in his treatment of the united monarchy. Dr. Davis has brought to the illumination of the historical record the contributions of many disciplines that are currently making fresh impact on Biblical studies. Attention to the sketch maps and line-drawn illustrations of military campaigns will reveal that he has given careful consideration to geography. Insights from comparative literature of the ancient Near East on social and political conditions contemporary with the monarchy have been employed to good effect. Information on the Philistines, presently being recovered by archaeological excavation, has influenced his presentation of their role in Biblical history.

While the interests and needs of the lay reader have been kept in mind throughout, Dr. Davis has not hesitated to deal with some of the vexing problems presented by the state of preservation of the Hebrew text. His conclusions in these matters are conservative and well-balanced. He has also addressed himself in appropriate places to problems of a nature sometimes theological, sometimes ethical, at other times historical or higher critical, all with measured good judgment. I am happy to observe that proper attention has also been directed toward devotional commentary, so that the work is not merely a technical treatment of historical record, but seeks to provide practical spiritual help as well.

I hope that this contribution from the pen of Dr. Davis will further a renewed interest in Bible history. God revealed Himself to and through Israel in the course of that nation's history, culminating in His own appearance in the flesh in the person of His Son. Hence if we are really interested in revelation, we will be interested in the inspired historical record. May this present work whet our appetite.

I-II SAMUEL

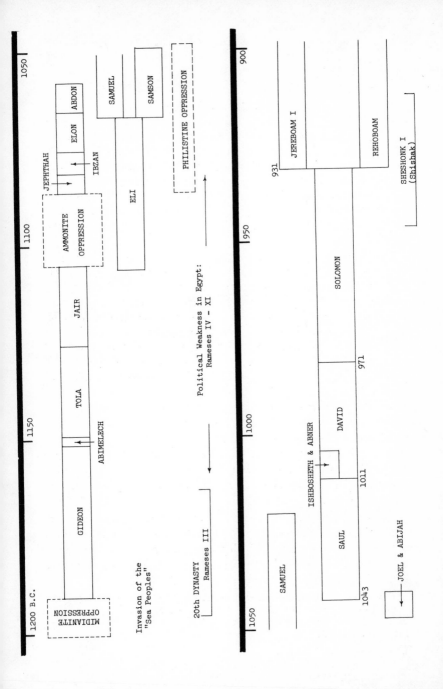

Chapter 1

INTRODUCTION

Triumph and tragedy are the two words which best describe the content of the books of Samuel. Some of Israel's greatest moments of glory and darkest hours of defeat are retold with simplicity and candor. The stories retold in these books are of significant value didactically for this present age. The faith and the failures of both great and small are viewed in the light of sovereign grace. Historically the books are masterpieces of national record.

The campaigns of Joshua conducted about 1400 B.C. enabled the children of Israel to occupy the hill country and certain sections of the lowlands. However, with that occupancy came the gradual infiltration of Caananitic social and religious practices. These had a tremendous negative effect on the progress of Israelite colonization. Due to the subtle infiltration of Baalism, the spiritual life of Israel very quickly degenerated into a state of apostasy.[1] The rise of divinely appointed judges during this period provided mainly for military needs. Under many of the judges there was a noticeable spiritual decline, and in many cases, this was either initiated or permitted by the judges themselves.[2] In addition to the internal strife and spiritual weakness there was increasing military pressure upon Israel from the outside. It was in this context that the prophet Samuel made his appearance, and a most important one it was. He was a very capable physician coming to the aid of Israel at a time when her fever was at the highest.

Before entering upon a study of the text of Samuel, it is imperative that the historical and cultural framework of the period of the United Monarchy be clearly established. The discussion that follows, therefore, will be devoted to a broad view of the na-

---

[1]For a full discussion of this era see John J. Davis, *Conquest and Crisis* (Grand Rapids: Baker Book House, 1969), p. 93.

[2]E.g. Gideon (Judg. 8:27-32), Jephthah (Judg. 11:30-40) and Samson (Judg. 14:1—16:31).

tion of Israel and her place in the ancient Near East during the
days of Samuel, Saul, David, and Solomon.

I. HISTORICAL SETTING

A. *The Biblical Data*

The historical framework for the books of Samuel is the eleventh and tenth centuries B.C. The chronology for this period is
established upon the date for the death of Solomon in 931/30
B.C.[3] The beginning of Solomon's reign would therefore fall in
the year 971/70 B.C. since he reigned for forty years (I Kings
11:42). According to I Kings 6:1 the construction of Solomon's
temple began in the fourth year of his reign (i.e., 967/66 B.C.).
II Samuel 5:4 states that David reigned for a period of forty
years, thus placing his coronation date in the year 1011 B.C.
The exact date for the beginning of Saul's reign is not so easily
established. The only information available to us is found in
Acts 13:21. There it is stated that Saul's reign lasted for a period
of forty years, thus placing the beginning of his reign in 1050
B.C. It is possible, however, that this figure includes the total
duration of his dynasty rather than his specific rule. If this were
the case, his reign would have begun in 1043 B.C., for Ish-bosheth lived seven years after the death of Saul and reigned part
of that time (cf. II Sam. 2:10-11).

The ministry of Samuel spanned the latter days of Samson,
Elon and Abdon and continued through most of the reign of
Saul (see chart, page 16).

B. *Egypt and Palestine*

1. *Egypt: The Twentieth Dynasty*

The last significant king of the Nineteenth Dynasty was Merneptah (1234-1222 B.C.) who was already an old man when he
came to the throne in 1234 B.C. His reign was marked by a
number of major invasions, the most notable of which was that
attempted by the Lybians. He claimed to have successfully re-

---

[3]Edwin J. Thiele, *The Mysterious Numbers of the Hebrew Kings* (Grand
Rapids: William B. Eerdmans Publishing Co., Revised edition, 1965), p. 53.

sisted this invasion and to have captured 9,000 prisoners.[4] The most interesting inscription attributed to the time of Merneptah is his famous victory stela in which Israel is mentioned. The account of his victories in Caanan reads as follows:

> The princes are saying: Mercy
> No one raises his head among the nine bows.
> Desolation is for Tehenu; Hatti is pacified;
> Plundered is the Caanan with every evil;
> Carried off is Ashkelon; seized upon is Gezer;
> Yanoam is made as that which does not exist;
> Israel is laid waste, his seed is not.[5]

That Israel was already in Palestine and had expanded its landholdings toward the west is implied by this inscription. The death of Merneptah initiated a period of political chaos in Egypt which lasted for some twenty years. During this time a number of usurpers succeeded in getting the throne, one of them even being a Syrian. The restoration of order and national unity was not achieved until Setnakht (1197-1195 B.C.) took the throne. This began the Twentieth Dynasty in Egypt. His son Ramses III (1195-1164 B.C.) was a strong and energetic king. During his reign the Lybians again made their presence felt and successfully infiltrated portions of the fertile Delta region. This clearly was a serious internal threat to the security of the rest of the country. In the fifth year of Ramses III a very bloody battle was conducted with the Lybians resulting in victory for this Pharaoh. With this victory the troubles of Ramses III had not ended, however. From the north there were ominous signs of another major power invasion by a people known in Egyptian documents as the "Sea Peoples" or "Peoples of the Sea." These too were defeated by Ramses III in a great battle, and this prevented the overthrow of the Delta region from the north. A very

---

[4]Francis D. Nichol, ed. "The Ancient World from c. 1400 to 586 B.C.," *The Seventh-day Adventist Bible Commentary* (Review and Herald Publishing Assoc., 1954), II, p. 26.

[5]James B. Pritchard, ed., *Ancient Near Eastern Texts*, "Hymn of Victory of Mer-ne-Ptah," trans. John A. Wilson (New Jersey: Princeton University Press, 1955), p. 378 (Hereafter referred to as *ANET.*).

vivid representation of this battle is found in the temple at
Medinet Habu.

Following the reign of Ramses III, Egypt once again went into a period of decline under Ramses IV through XI. The high
priests of Amun were gaining significant political and economic
power in Egypt. At the end of the Twentieth Dynasty (ca.
1085 B.C.) Egypt was at its lowest point. The Twenty-first Dynasty in Egypt was also a period of considerable confusion and
weakness. Kings came from families of the high priests at Kar-
nak, and princes of Tanis. One of the results of this period of
weakness and internal strife was the loss of prestige in Palestine.
This phenomenon is reflected in the story of Wen-Amon and
his journey to Byblos as an Egyptian envoy.[6]

2. Palestine

The materials which best reflect the historical-cultural context
of the United Monarchy come to us from two archaeological
periods known as Iron Age I (1200-900 B.C.) and Iron Age II
(900-550 B.C.). The Iron Age I period was politically dominated by the presence of the Philistines along the coast lands
and in portions of the Esdraelon Valley, and as far east as the
Jordan Valley.[7] Their power was centered, however, in five
cities in southwestern Palestine. These were Ashkelon, Ashdod,
Ekron, Gaza, and Gath (I Sam. 6:17). Each city was ruled by a
"lord" (Heb. seren). One of the secrets to Philistine military success was their effective use of iron. About 1200 B.C. the Philistines introduced it to Palestine for common use. Prior to this
time the Hittites used iron quite widely in Asia Minor. The
monopoly of the iron smelting process was a decided advantage
to the Philistines in keeping Israel weak and on the defensive
militarily (cf. I Sam. 13:19-22). It was not until the time of
David that this monopoly was successfully broken, and Israel
achieved the military strength necessary to occupy portions of
the Philistine's territory. The Iron I period was also character-

---

    [6]ANET, "The Journey of Wen-Amon to Phoenicia," trans. John A. Wil-
son, pp. 25-29.
    [7]G. Ernest Wright, "Fresh Evidence for the Philistine Story," The Bibli-
cal Archaeology, XXIX, 3, (Sept., 1966), p. 74.

Clay Lamp from Iron Age I (1200-900 B.C.). Levant Photo Service

ized by an absence of Israelite sanctuaries. According to Albright, very few amulets dating to this period have been discovered in Israelite cities.[8] Philistine burial customs are known to us from the discovery of a number of anthropoid clay coffins.[9] The pottery of the Philistines was quite distinctive. Most characteristic of the decorations were metopes enclosing stylized birds, very often with the head turned back (see illus., p. 27). These motifs show affinity with typical patterns found on pottery from the Aegean area. Philistine jugs were usually provided with a strainer spout, probably intended to drain out the barley husk from beer.[10] The clay lamps from the Iron Age I period became a little more shallow. The rims on the outside were flat

[8]William F. Albright, *The Archaeology of Palestine* (Baltimore: Penguin Books, 1961), p. 120.

[9]G. Ernest Wright, "Philistine Coffins and Mercenaries," *The Biblical Archaeologist*, XXII, 3, (Sept. 1959).

[10]William F. Albright, *op. cit.*, p. 115.

or flared at the back, and the pinching effect in the front was far more pronounced and deeper (see illus., p. 21). The city walls of this period were generally constructed after the casemate pattern. Casemate walls were double walls with a space in between and supported by a series of buttresses at regular intervals.

The Iron Age II period (900-550 B.C.) includes the period of the Divided Monarchy. Many very significant written documents have come to us from this period, such as the famous Gezer calendar discovered in 1908.[11] Also included in this important body of written documents are the Samaria Ostrara,[12] the Lachish Ostraca,[13] and the Siloam inscription.[14] Objects from this period tend to be standardized to a high degree perhaps due to the development of mass production techniques. Vast amounts of information have come to us from Samaria, Megiddo, Lachish, Tell Beit Mirsim, Tell en-Nasbeh, Tell el-Far'ah, and Hazor regarding the material culture of this period. In 1968 work was begun at the important site of Tekoa, and one rather large tomb excavated under the supervision of the author yielded a fine selection of pottery from this period. The wall and gate systems of important cities are now well documented. More recent studies have shed light on water systems from this period.[15]

C. *Other Nations*

One of the more serious threats to Israel's expansion policy

[11]ANET, "The Gezer Calendar," trans. W. F. Albright, p. 320.

[12]D. Winton Thomas, *Documents from Old Testament Times* (New York: Harper & Brothers, 1961), pp. 204-208.

[13]*Ibid.* pp. 212-217. Also of importance is the fine collection of ostraca found at Tell Arad, "During the five seasons of excavation, over 200 ostraca were found, nearly half Aramaic (from approximately 400 B.C.) and the rest Hebrew, from the time of the monarchy." Yohanan Aharoni, "Arad: Its Inscriptions and Temple," *The Biblical Archaeologist,* XXXI, 1 (Feb., 1968), p. 9. See also Y. Aharoni, "Hebrew Ostraca from Tel Arad," *Israel Exploration Journal,* XVI, 1 (1966), pp. 1-7.

[14]D. Winton Thomas, *op. cit.,* pp. 209-211.

[15]Yigael Yadin, "The Fifth Season of Excavations at Hazor," *The Biblical Archaeologist,* XXXII, 3 (1969), pp. 63 ff., and William G. Dever, "The Water Systems at Hazor and Gezer," *ibid.*

under her early kings came from a territory to the north known as Aram (AV, "Syria"). In the century or so before the rise of the Hebrew monarchy, these people gradually gained control of the territory from Haran in northern Mesopotamia, west to the Lebanon Mountains, to the Taurus Mountains in the north, and beyond Damascus on the south. One of the most significant of the Aramean states was known as Zobah, located north of Damascus (cf. II Sam. 8:3-9).[16]

The Hittite empire between 1400 and 1200 B.C. was of considerable significance as evidenced in both Hittite and Egyptian literature. However, about 1200 B.C. the Hittite empire came to a catastrophic and immediate end. This was most likely caused by the mass movement of "Sea Peoples" known to us from Egyptian documents and Palestinian archaeology. Also important to the history of this period was the rise and decline of Assyria. Complete independence came under Ashur-uballit I (1375-1340 B.C.). Prior to this time Assyria appears to have been subject to Mitanni. One of the more significant kings of this period of Assyrian rise was Tiglath-pileser I (1115-1102 B.C.). His reign was characterized by consistent, ruthless campaigning. He successfully campaigned to the Black Sea in the north and the Mediterranean on the west. Only a Babylonian revolt saved Palestine from Assyrian aggression at this time. After the death of Tiglath-pileser I, Assyria went into a period of general decline, thus preventing any major encounter with the rising empire of King David.

The only other enemies that existed during this period of time consisted of smaller nations to the east and the south of Israel. These were the Edomites, Amalekites, Moabites, and Ammonites. In many cases these nations were defeated by Saul, but it was not until the time of David that their territories were occupied and successfully controlled on a long-term basis. Generally speaking, therefore, the stage was set and prepared for the rise of the Hebrew monarchy.

---

[16]For a more complete discussion of this subject, see Merrill F. Unger, *Israel and the Aramaeans of Damascus* (London: James Clarke & Co., LTD, 1951).

II. THE BIBLICAL RECORD

A. *The Title of the Books*

The two books of Samuel were originally one. It was not until
the third century B.C. that the translators of the Septuagint
divided the book into two portions. The Vulgate followed this
division, and it has been adopted in almost all translations since.
The translators of the Septuagint called I and II Samuel the first
and second books of the Kingdoms; the two books of Kings were
then known as the third and fourth books of the Kingdoms. This
two-fold division of the books of Samuel was first introduced into
the Hebrew text by the Venetian printer Daniel Bomberg in his
first edition of the Hebrew Bible, dated 1516.

The books get their title from the prophet Samuel, the principal character of the opening chapters. In view of the fact that
he was the last of the judges, one of the greatest prophets,
founder of the schools of the prophets, and the one who anointed
both Saul and David, it is not inappropriate that these books
bear his name.

B. *Position in the Canon*

The Hebrew Old Testament is divided into three sections
known as the Law (*tôrāh*), the Prophets (*Neḇî'îm*), and the
Writings (*keṯūḇîm*). The Law consists of the five books of Moses. The Prophets are divided into two sections — the former
and the latter (see chart below). The books of Samuel are included in that section known as the Former Prophets. The
Writings contain the poetical books, the five rolls, and some historical books.

Law	Prophets		Writings	
Five Books of Moses	Former Josh. — Kings	Latter Isa. — Mal.	Poetical Five Rolls Historical	(3 Books) (5 Books) (3 Books)

C. Authorship

Most liberal critics hold one of two views with regard to the sources of the books of Samuel. Many follow Robert Pfeiffer in citing two principal sources for these books: J and E. Others follow Eissfeldt who specifies three sources: L, J, and E. Some parts of the books of Samuel are held to be Solomonic while other parts are considered to be later editions dating about 550 B.C. by a redactor of the Deuteronomic school. Both of these theories of composition, however, have been shown to have been inadequate and in most cases improbable.[17]

According to the Talmud, Samuel was the author of Judges, Ruth, and the first part of Samuel. The remainder of I Samuel and II Samuel were supposedly composed by Nathan and Gad (I Chron. 29:29). This view, however, was questioned by Jewish commentators at a very early date. There are indications that large portions of the books must have been written after the death of Samuel (cf. I Sam. 25:1 and 28:3), and even after the division of the kingdom (I Sam. 27:6). The author of the books as we have them today is, therefore, unknown. In all probability a prophet, most likely from Judah, who lived after the division of the kingdom, composed these books incorporating earlier materials. The author would have made use of existing books such as the "Book of Jasher" (II Sam. 1:18) and the records of the "acts of David" (I Chron. 29:29).

D. Literary Quality and Text

Regardless of authorship, the narratives contained in the books of Samuel are masterpieces of historical writing. They represent the maximum achievement in the area of ancient historiography, for both the principal and the minor individuals are included in the narratives. These books present us with a gallery of historical portraits that are incomparable. Nowhere else in contem-

[17]See R. K. Harrison, *Introduction to the Old Testament* (Grand Rapids: William B. Eerdmans Publishing Co., 1969), pp. 696-709, and Gleason L. Archer, *A Survey of Old Testament Introduction* (Chicago: Moody Press, 1964), p. 272.

porary ancient Near Eastern literature do we have such personal
profiles as those contained in the books of Samuel.

The text of these books, however, comes to us in a state of
comparatively poor preservation. The exact reason for this is not
known to us at this point. Some of the problems with regard to
the transmission of the text have been solved by study of the
Dead Sea Scrolls. Other problems are still beyond solution at
this point,[18] but none are of such a serious nature as to impair
the basic theme and flow of the narrative.

E. *Purpose and Major Themes*

The principal purpose of these books is to provide an official
account of the ministry of Samuel along with the rise and development of the monarchy through the days of King David.
The transition from a theocracy to a monarchy is a crucial one in
Hebrew history; therefore, these books merit careful study. The
books of Samuel also emphasize several important theological
themes which should be noted. (1) There is the rejection of the
theocracy and its consequences, politically and spiritually. (2)
These books provide us with a unique study of the ministry of
the Holy Spirit within the framework of monarchial rule. (3)
The books also give insight into sin and its effects in the human
heart. (4) The development of the prophetic office and the
phenomonon of prophetism are described in many ways.

III. BASIC OUTLINE: I AND II SAMUEL

A. *Samuel: Judge and Prophet* (I Sam. 1:1–7:17)
   1. The Birth of Samuel (1:1–2:10)
   2. The Childhood of Samuel (2:11–3:21)
   3. The Capture and Return of the Ark (4:1–7:17)
B. *The Reign of Saul* (I Sam. 8:1–14:52)
   1. Israel's Demand for a King (chap. 8)
   2. Saul's Appointment and Anointing (9:1–10:27)
   3. Victory at Jabesh-Gilead (11:1-15)

---

[18]Further discussion of these problems and suggested solutions can be
found in R. K. Harrison, *op. cit.*, p. 697 ff. and G. L. Archer, *op. cit.*, p.
273.

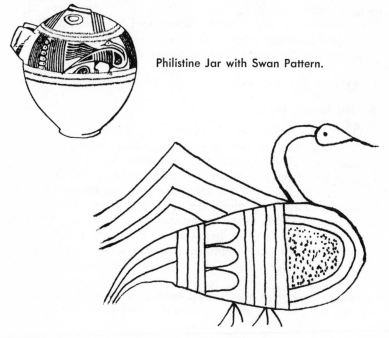

Philistine Jar with Swan Pattern.

A Bird, as Painted on a Philistine Jar.

Chapter 2

SAMUEL: JUDGE AND PROPHET
(I Samuel 1–7)

Out of the confusion and turmoil of the period of the judges arises one of the great figures of Old Testament history, the prophet Samuel. His appearance in this time of religious degeneracy and political distress was no accident of history. With the death of Samson, the country was disunited and leaderless. The Philistines were achieving greater strength and realizing significant victories as they directed their campaigns to the east. Corruption in the priesthood and moral scandals in connection with tabernacle worship (I Sam. 2:22) rendered the nation of Israel weak and impotent. This was also a time of very limited prophetic influence (I Sam. 3:1).

It was at this point that a ray of hope appeared through the ominous black clouds of disaster. God placed His hand on a young lady who was without children and heartbroken. It was the faith and the prayers of this inconspicuous figure that brought about a turning point in the events described above.

I. THE BIRTH OF SAMUEL (1:1–2:11)

A. *His Family Background* (1:1-9)

The father of Samuel is introduced in I Samuel 1:1. He is identified as Elkanah from Ramathaim-zophim in the mountains of Ephraim. The name Ramathaim-zophim literally means "two high places of the watchman," or "twin heights of the Zuphites." The exact location of Ramathaim-zophim is not known for sure. Three sites have been suggested: (1) *Beit Rima*, about twelve miles west of Shiloh in the mountains of Ephraim; (2) *Er-Ram*, about five miles north of Jerusalem in Benjamite territory; (3) Ramallah, in the mountains of Ephraim approximately eight miles north of Jerusalem.[19] Elkanah, like Gideon (Judg. 8:30-

---

[19]See Francis D. Nichol, *op. cit.*, pp. 548 ff. for a discussion of these sites and their value as candidates for the site of ancient Ramathaim-zophim.

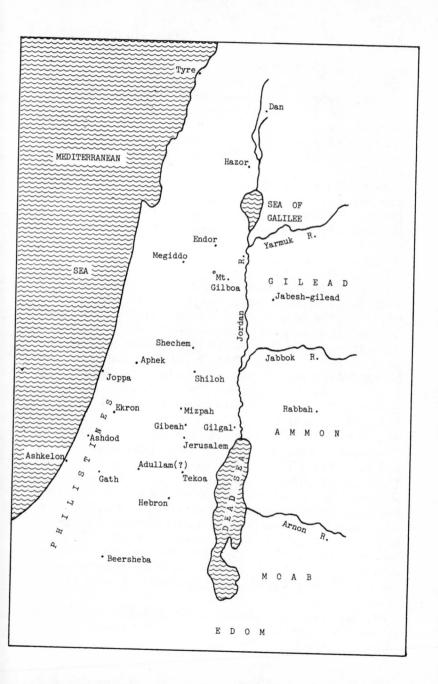

31) and Jair (Judg. 10:3-4), was a polygamist. With polygamy came trouble as was always the case in Biblical history. The one wife, Peninnah, bore him several children, but Hannah was barren despite her devotion to God (vv. 2, 5, 6). It was Elkanah's custom to go to Shiloh annually to worship the Lord at the tabernacle. Pilgrimages to Shiloh were required at least three times yearly according to Exodus 23:14-17 and Deuteronomy 16:16. Each year Hannah was given a "worthy portion" (v. 5), better translated "a double portion" (Heb. *mānāh 'aḥaṯ 'apāyim*). The great sorrow and disappointment of Hannah is reflected in the tragic words of verse 8 where her experiences at Shiloh were characterized by weeping, fasting and heaviness of heart.[20]

B. *Hannah's Vow* (1:10-23)

In great bitterness of soul (v. 10; cf. II Kings 4:27) she prayed to the Lord and the essence of this prayer is wrapped up in two words found in verse 11, "remember me." These words have a familiar ring to them. They represent the prayer of a soul in desperate need. One is reminded of the simplicity of Samson's prayer recorded in Judges 16:28. In blindness and helplessness he cried out to his God and asked to be "remembered." This prayer was also found on the lips of a man being crucified at Calvary. One of the malefactors who was hanged with Jesus looked to Him with faith and said, "Lord, *remember me* when thou comest into thy kingdom" (Luke 23:42). The sincerity and the simplicity of this plea were quickly recognized by the Lord, and He replied, "To day shalt thou be with me in paradise" (Luke 23:42). Hannah vowed that if a son were given to her, she would dedicate him as a lifelong Nazarite (v. 11). Only two other lifelong Nazarites are mentioned in Scripture: Samson (Judg. 13, 14) and John the Baptist (Luke 1:15). The requirements for a Nazarite were threefold: (1) the abstinence from wine (Num. 6:3-4); (2) letting the hair grow untouched by a razor (Num. 6:5); (3) refraining from ceremonial defilement by touching a dead body (Num. 6:6). A fragment from

---

[20]The expression "better than ten sons" was evidently a common idiom meaning "large family" (cf. Ruth 4:15).

SAMUEL: JUDGE AND PROPHET

the book of Samuel found in the fourth cave at Khirbet Qumran specifically states that Samuel was a Nazarite.

Eli, the priest, mistook Hannah for one who was drunk with wine, in that she moved her lips but did not make audible sounds (cf. vv. 12 ff.). She quickly denied the charge that she was a drunkard and pled that she should not be counted as a "daughter of Belial" (v. 16, Heb. *baṯ belîyā'al*). To be regarded in this manner was to be given an extremely low and degraded position. The expression, "the sons of Belial," is commonly found in the Old Testament and is associated with idolatry (Deut. 13: 13), rebellion (I Sam. 2:12), lewd and sensuous acts (Judg. 19: 22; 20:13), arrogance and stupidity (I Sam. 25:17), and murder (I Kings 21:13). The Hebrew expression "Belial" literally means "without profit or value." Upon hearing Hannah's explanation, he assured her of blessing and sent her away in peace (v. 17). Notice the composing influence of prayer in the life of this individual. Whereas she was unable to eat previously (v. 8), she now was able to eat and her countenance was changed (v. 18). As a result of her faith and obedience, the Lord "remembered her" (v. 19). In due time a child was born and was given the name Samuel, which has been variously interpreted to mean "name of God" (Heb. *šēm +'ēl*), "his name is God" (Heb. *šemo +'ēl*), "heard of God" (Heb. *šemûa'+'ēl*)

C. *Hannah's Obedience* (1:24-28)

After the child was weaned, which would have been two or possibly three years,[21] he was taken to the tabernacle at Shiloh and, after appropriate sacrifices were offered (vv. 24-25), dedicated to the service of the Lord.

D. *Hannah's Praise* (2:1-11)

This chapter stands in contrast to the events recorded in Chapter 1. There Hannah appeared on the scene in the deepest of grief and with a broken heart (1:8). In this chapter, however, she stands high with a heart that rejoices and praises her God

---

[21]Cf. II Macc. 7:27.

because of victory (2:1). The prayer itself is in contrast to the prayer of Chapter 1. There she prayed in bitterness and wept (1:10). In this chapter her voice is that of a victor rejoicing in God's blessing (2:1). Four stanzas, or themes, are apparent in this short prayer. The first is characterized by thanksgiving and praise (vv. 1-2). The second (v. 3) is a severe warning to those who are arrogant and proud. The third includes verses 4 through 8 and speaks about the humiliation of those who are lofty and the elevation of those who are humble and lowly. The final stanza is an expression of confidence as she looked toward the future (2:9-10). The prayer of Hannah exhibits considerable theological insight and knowledge of the Pentateuch. For example, the *holiness* of God is emphasized in verse 2, and the *knowledge* of God in verse 3. In the remaining verses the *power* of God is quite evident. Especially interesting is the expression in verse 10, "and he shall give strength unto his king, and exalt the horn of his anointed." Even though Israel did not have a king at this time, such was anticipated, for Moses had prophesied of a king (Duet. 17:14). The expression "anointed" could be applied to priests (Lev. 4:3), prophets (I Kings 19:16) as well as to kings. It might well, however, point to the future Messiah who would be the King of kings. Hannah's song recorded in this chapter appears to be the basis of Mary's *Magnificat* found in Luke 1:46-55.

II. THE CHILDHOOD OF SAMUEL (2:12—3:21)

A. *Corruption in the Priesthood* (2:12-17)

The real tragedy of those days cannot be fully appreciated until one carefully studies the verses that follow. The sons of Eli are described as "sons of Belial" (cf. 2:12). The sons of Eli clearly reflected the conditions of the times in which they lived. They were very much a part of the apostasy of the age of the judges. They, in fact, were openly stealing from God (vv. 13-17). The priest was only allowed to take the breast and right thigh as his share of the sacrifice (Lev. 7:34). He was not to take this share until the meat had been properly offered to God. In the light of these facts, it should be observed that the sin of

Hophni and Phinehas was threefold: (a) They took any part of the meat they wished to have (2:13-14). (b) They took the meat before it had been offered to the Lord (2:14-15). (c) They took it by force (2:16). In contrast to this dark and discouraging situation was the faith and obedience of Elkanah and his family (vv. 18-21). They returned to Shiloh faithfully to worship their God, and the Lord honored this faith by giving to Hannah additional children (v. 21).

The writer then turns our attention again to the sons of Eli who, in addition to destroying proper sacrificial procedures, also brought shame and immorality to the central sanctuary (v. 22). These actions, at least for Phinehas, may have meant open adultery (cf. 4:19). The moral and spiritual effects of these acts were widespread in Israel (2:24), resulting in more sin and corruption among the leaders (4:3; 8:1-5). It also resulted in a breakdown in the people's faithfulness to the law of Moses (cf. I Sam. 14:32). These sons had become so hardened in their deeds that they completely refused counsel and rebuke from their father (v. 25). Such rebuke, however, may have been very mild and perhaps very late in life (cf. 3:13). The lack of paternal restraint is quite clearly one of the causes of delinquency of these young men. A prophet was sent to the sanctuary to bring warning to Eli and to prophesy the death of his sons (vv. 27-36). The death of Hophni and Phinehas was a sign of God's displeasure and judgment upon Eli's household (v. 34). But the Lord promised to raise up a "faithful priest" who would follow His ways and walk in accordance with His revealed will.

B. *The Identity of the Faithful Priest* (2:35)

The precise interpretation of this verse has been subject to considerable discussion on the part of scholars throughout the years. The promise of a perpetual priesthood was first given to Aaron, a descendant of Levi, the son of Jacob (Exod. 28:43; 29:9). This promise was, of course, made to Aaron and his house generally. It was because of the sacrilegious acts of Nadab and Abihu in offering "strange fire" (Lev. 10:1-2; Num. 3:4) that they "died before Jehovah." They had no children; so Eleazar, the third son of Aaron, and his younger brother, Ithamar, occupied a more important position, for they "ministered in the priest's office in the presence of Aaron their father" (Num. 3:4; I Chron. 24:1-2).

When Aaron died, Eleazar, the oldest living son, became the high priest (Num. 20:22-29). Later the priesthood was given to Phinehas, the son of Eleazar, "because he was zealous for his God, and made atonement for the children of Israel" (Num. 25:11-13). Due to some unexplained cause, the high priesthood was transferred from the line of Eleazar to that of Ithamar in the person of Eli. The book of Samuel begins with Eli as high priest, and there is no hint that Eli's claim to the priesthood was a false one or one which he usurped in an improper manner.

The context at hand indicates that with the death of Hophni and Phinehas a faithful priest would arise who would fulfill the will of God (vv. 34-35). A number of views are held by commentators with regard to the identity of this faithful priest. Some feel that this prophecy was fulfilled in the "whole house of Aaron."[22] Spence, on the other hand, argued that Samuel fulfilled the requirements of that verse.[23] Renwick asserts that the "faithful priest" was only completely fulfilled in Christ, although it had a partial reference to Samuel.[24] The preferable view seems to be that which considers the prophecy as fulfilled in the accession of the priest Zadok and his family to the office in the time of Solomon. When I Kings 2:26-27 is examined in the light of I Samuel 14:3 and 22:20, it is clear that the house of Eli continued until the days of Solomon. Then God transferred the high priesthood back to the line of Eleazar, in the person of Zadok, who remained faithful to David at the time of Adonijah's rebellion (I Kings 1:7-8). This prophecy also indicates that there will never lack a descendant of Zadok to walk before God's

[22]C. F. Keil and F. Delitzsch, *Biblical Commentary on the Books of Samuel*, trans. James Martin (Grand Rapids: William B. Eerdmans Publishing Co., 1950), pp. 40-43.

[23]H. D. M. Spence, "I Samuel," *Ellicott's Commentary on the Whole Bible*, Charles Ellicott, ed. (Grand Rapids: Zondervan Publishing House, n.d.), p. 303.

[24]A. M. Renwick, "I and II Samuel," *The New Bible Commentary*, F. Davidson, A. M. Stibbs and E. F. Kevan, eds. (Grand Rapids: William B. Eerdmans Publishing Co., 1953), p. 265.

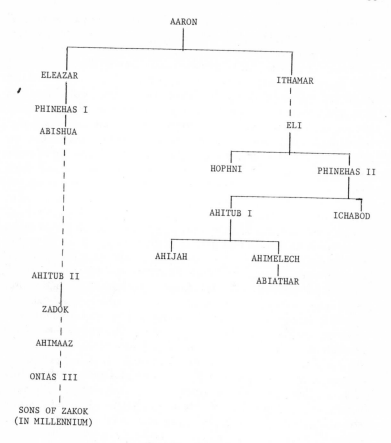

The Line of Aaron

anointed kings. Zadok himself walked before David and Solomon, and the sons of Zadok will walk before Christ in the millennial temple (Ezek. 44:15; 48:11; cf. Jer. 33:21).

C. *Encounter with the Lord* (3:1-21)

The call of Samuel recorded in this chapter is rather unique. Apostasy and prophetic inactivity characterized those days. Literally translated, the latter part of verse 1 reads, "The word

of the Lord was scarce in those days; vision was not common."
There were evidently very few men who were willing to follow
the Lord and proclaim His revelation. A notable exception is
recorded in 2:27 ff. Eli at this time was very old (v. 2), and his
sons were extremely corrupt. It appeared that there was little
hope for religious revival in Israel under those conditions. It
was during the early morning hours that the Lord spoke audibly
to Samuel (cf. v. 3).[25] The audible call of Samuel was somewhat unique in reference to prophetic revelation (cf. Num. 12:
6). Because of the inability of Eli to see (v. 2), Samuel perhaps
assumed that it was he who was calling in order to get some
help. After several occurrences of this experience, Eli recognized
that the voice was that of the Lord, and recommended that Samuel respond accordingly (v. 9). The first charge given to Samuel
was not an easy one to carry out. It was one which would make
"the ears of everyone that hear it tingle" (v. 11; cf. II Kings 21:
12 and Jer. 19:3). He had to bring to Eli the sad tidings of
divine judgment upon his household (vv. 13-14). This, indeed,
was a most difficult task for Samuel who had spent many precious years with Eli. The tension of the situation is revealed in
verse 15. This was, indeed, the first great test for Samuel. He,
however, weighed the issues and realized the importance of his
message and told all to Eli in obedience to God's command (vv.
18 ff.). This valor and commitment brought blessing to the life
of Samuel as it always does to the man of God who faithfully
conveys God's message, whether it is of judgment or blessing.
In fact, one of the marks of a true prophet was that he was not
ashamed or afraid to reveal the essential needs of God's people
(Mic. 3:7-8).

III. DEFEAT AND SHAME (4:1–7:17)

After the death of Samson (about the middle of the eleventh
century B.C.), the Philistines were able to regroup their military

---

[25]The "lamp of God" is a reference to the candlestick in the tabernacle.
The seven lamps were lighted every evening and burned until the oil was
consumed the next morning (Exod. 38:8; Lev. 24:2; II Chron. 13:11; Exod.
27:21). The reference, therefore, is to the period just before the morning
dawn.

units and once again attempt penetration into Israelite-controlled territory. The Philistines not only played an important military role with respect to Palestine at this time, but as previously noted they encountered Merneptah and Ramses III in the Delta region of Egypt. The Philistines were, in fact, one of a number of tribes known in Egyptian sources as "Peoples of the Sea," which was a collective name for eight tribes which participated in the invasion of Egypt. The migration of Sea Peoples from Crete and the Aegean was not a new phenomenon. In the Pentateuch we read of "Philistines" who had settled along the southwest coast of Palestine (see Gen. 21:34; 26:1; Exod. 13:17-18). The Minoan settlers who had been in Palestine for centuries never achieved independent military strength as noted in the treaties they sought with Abraham and Isaac (Gen. 21:22-32; 26:26-33). However, when the Philistines and other tribes among the Peoples of the Sea joined these Minoan settlements, they formed a rather strong political and military organization. The Philistines were, therefore, the greatest menace to Israelite security during the days of Samuel.

The Philistines saw this time as a golden opportunity for invasion. Israel was badly divided and lacked religious and military leadership. A major battle took place in the area of Aphek (v. 1) where the Philistines were decisive victors, as indicated by the death of 4,000 Israelite troops (v. 2). When the Israelites assessed the situation, they concluded that the reason for failure was the absence of the Ark of the Covenant in their midst (v. 3). They had evidently assumed that the secret to the crossing of the Jordan (Josh. 3:11) and the victory at Jericho (Josh. 6:7, 8, 13) were due to the presence of the Ark. Their view of the Ark at this point appears to be somewhat superstitious, if not idolatrous. The two sons of Eli fully agreed to this plan and took the Ark to the camp of the Hebrews, which resulted in great rejoicing among the troops (vv. 5-6). The next battle was even more disastrous for Israel than the previous one, for again the Philistines were victorious and slew 30,000 footmen among the children of Israel (v. 10). But that was not the only tragedy on that occasion. The two sons of Eli were slain, and the precious Ark of the Covenant was taken into captivity (v. 11). The news of the death of Hophni and Phinehas, along

with the capture of the Ark, was too much for Eli and resulted
in his death (v. 18). At that time Phinehas' wife gave birth to a
child who was given the name I-chabod. Some translate this
name as meaning "Where is the glory?" However, a better rendering of the Hebrew *'īkābod* would be "no glory." This first
element in the compound name *'ī* is an ancient negative particle
used in a number of names. The departure of the Ark meant the
absence of glory in Israel (v. 22).

The journey of the Ark of the Covenant is a most interesting
one (see map). The Ark was first taken to the city of Ashdod
which appears to have been a rather important commercial
center in the Iron Age period.[26] The mound has some twenty
occupational levels ranging from the Early Bronze Age
to the Byzantine period. Tablets from the city of Ugarit men-

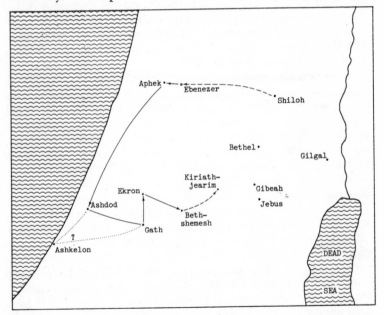

The Journey of the Ark

[26]See David N. Freedman, "The Second Season at Ancient Ashdod," *The
Biblical Archaeologist*, XXVI, 4, (Dec., 1963), p. 134 ff.

tion the fact that shipments of linen came from Ashdod. Some of the walls from the Philistine period still stand to a height of seven feet. It is clear, therefore, that Ashdod was an important city to the Philistines. The Biblical account confirms this observation in mentioning the presence of a temple dedicated to one of the principal Philistine deities, Dagon. The term "Dagon" has been traced to two Hebrew roots. One suggestion is that it comes from *dāg* meaning "fish." Supporting this theory are a number of coins found at Ashkelon, having an image of a deity that was apparently half man and half fish. A better view, however, traces the term to *dāgān* which means "grain." Evidently this deity was an important fertility god among the Philistines and perhaps among the peoples of Ugarit. In Ugaritic literature, Baal is referred to as the "son of Dagon."[27] From the information gathered in Chapters 5 and 6 it appears that the Philistines had developed a rather sophisticated religious system including a temple (5:2), a priesthood (6:2), religious "diviners" (6:2), and some concept of an "offering" (6:3-4).

When the Ark reached Ashdod, it was an object of tremendous attention. To capture the most sacred object of the enemy was, indeed, a great achievement. However, the Ark brought to Ashdod and its temple shame and humiliation along with a serious plague. According to verse 6 the Lord plagued the people of Ashdod with emrods (Heb. *'apōlîm* – "boils"). Many feel that this is one of the first references to "the black death," or bubonic plague. This is inferred from the mention of tumors and mice (possibly rats) that "marred the land" (cf. 5:6; 6:4-5). The exhibition of the Ark at Ashdod was hardly a credit or an asset to that city. With considerable dispatch and speed it was moved to the city of Gath (v. 8) where a similar tragedy occurred. From there the Ark was taken to Ekron and the plague followed it there.

After seven months (6:1) the Philistines realized the cause of their humiliation and sickness. The priests and the diviners suggested that the Ark be immediately returned to Israel and that it

---

[27]*ANET*, "Poems about Baal and Anath," trans. H. L. Ginsberg, C (I) III ABB, p. 130; h. IAB, p. 140; IV ABIII, p. 142, and "The Legend of King Keret," KRT A (ii), p. 143.

should be accompanied with a "trespass offering" (v. 3). The "golden mice" mentioned in 6:4 demonstrates that the Philistines believed in what is commonly known as "sympathetic magic," that is, the removal of evil or disaster *via* models. The Ark was returned to the Israelite city of Beth-shemesh (v. 9) and here another tragedy befell the men of that city. This was occasioned by their disobedience and mishandling of the Ark. The men of Beth-shemesh were really without excuse in their presumptuous sin of looking into the Ark. In the first place, Beth-shemesh was a priestly city (Josh. 21:16) and certainly had proper orientation as to the handling of the Ark. Second, there were Levites present on this occasion who certainly knew the penalty of mishandling the Ark. God had given clear instructions on this matter to Moses (Num. 4:5-6, 15-20).

It is doubtful that the number "50,000" belongs in the text. In the first place, the syntax is irregular in that there is an absence of the conjunction and the small number comes first. Second, three reputable manuscripts omit that number. Third, it is highly improbable that 50,000 people lived in that small community. Fourth, Josephus states that 70 died and does not mention the 50,000 (*Antiquities* 6:1:4).[28]

After the judgment at Beth-shemesh the Ark was then taken to Kirjath-jearim (7:2) where it remained for a considerable period of time. There are a number of explanations offered as to why the Ark was returned here and not to Shiloh. Some suggest it was a sign of the apostasy of the period. Others feel that the carrying away of the Ark and its removal from Shiloh was, in effect, a judgment and the people were not permitted to return it. The best explanation, however, comes from archaeological data. A Danish expedition excavated the site of Shiloh between 1923 and 1931 and demonstrated that Shiloh, while occupied from the thirteenth to the eleventh centuries B.C., was probably destroyed approximately 1050 B.C.[29]

Following these events, Samuel gathered all Israel together at

---

[28]For further discussion of this problem see John J. Davis, *Biblical Numerology* (Grand Rapids: Baker Book House, 1968), pp. 87-89.

[29]See Millar Burrows, *What Mean These Stones?* (New York: Meridian Books, 1957), p. 80.

Mizpeh (Tell en-Nasbeh), located about seven miles north of Jerusalem. The people, who had now put away their strange gods, were ready to listen to the spiritual counsel of Samuel (cf. vv. 3-5). Samuel promised to pray for the people (v. 5), a practice for which he was well known (cf. 8:6; 12:19, 23). Samuel preached at Mizpeh and the people confessed their sin. The Philistines noted this return to unity and spiritual commitment and considered it a serious threat to their own security (v. 7). Samuel assured the people of Israel that victory would be theirs if they would trust in their God for power. When the Israelites encountered the Philistine armies for the third major battle, they were given victory which was rather decisive (cf. vv. 13-14).

One would expect a continued revival and spiritual growth among the people who had experienced such a reversal in political and military trends; however, such was not the case. As the Philistines and Ammonites began to apply additional pressure on the borders of Israel, rather than turning to God, the children of Israel sought out a human leader to provide military victory.

Chapter 3

SAUL: RUSTIC WARRIOR AND KING
(I Samuel 8—12)

Frustration and despair have a way of distorting human perspectives to such a degree that rash and ofttimes hasty decisions are made, which are later regretted. In the days of Samuel the nation had gone through many moments of military and social anguish. The shame of national defeat was more than Israel could continue to bear. It was out of these conditions that Israel decided that the solution to her problem was the establishment of a monarchy.

I. ISRAEL'S DEMAND FOR A KING (8:1-10)

As Samuel grew older he placed his sons in important positions of legal authority (vv. 1-2). His sons, like the sons of Eli, did not follow his ways. These young men were easily turned aside by bribes, thus perverting and distorting the basic elements of proper judgment (v. 3). The corruption of the priesthood, the lack of honest deportment among the judges and the advanced age of Samuel caused the elders of Israel to approach Samuel at Ramah (v. 4) demanding a king. At least three reasons were given by the elders for their decision on this matter: (1) They wanted to prevent further military losses (cf. 8:20;

Ramah (Er Ram), the home town of the prophet Samuel (I Sam. 1:19; 2:11; 7:17). Matson Photo Service

12:12). In previous battles with the Philistines over 34,000 men lost their lives (4:2, 10). In addition to this, two sons of the high priest were slain and the Ark had been taken by the Philistines and kept for seven months. (2) Because of corruption among Israel's leaders (cf. 2:12-17; 8:3, 5). The sons of Eli and the sons of Samuel were complete failures and merely compounded the frustration of Israel rather than giving hope for the future. The leaders perhaps felt that a tribal confederacy under the leadership of divinely appointed judges was not the best answer to their immediate problems. They, perhaps, looked back on the three hundred years that had gone by with various degrees of success and failure. In all probability, they looked at the failures during the times of the judges and attributed those failures to the political organization rather than to national apostasy. (3) They wanted to be like the other nations (8:5, 20). This viewpoint reflected a serious problem in the spiritual and moral consciousness of the nation. This completely reversed God's design for His people who were chosen to be holy and separate (Lev. 20:26). Through the series of miracles in Egypt, God intended to make a clear difference between Israel and Egypt (cf. Exod. 11:7). Because Israel had failed in the total conquest of Canaan, she now took the direction of political compatibility and assumed that this would care for the problems of oppression and military failure.

While these were the formal reasons given to Samuel to establish a monarchy, a careful study of Israel's attitudes during this period of time indicates that there were other underlying motives: (a) They rejected the theocracy, which God recognized immediately (cf. 8:7). (b) They had serious interests in materialistic success. This is indicated in the first chapter of Judges. When the tribes had the ability to drive out the enemy, they instead put them to task work in order to improve their economic status (cf. Judg. 1:28, 30, 33). It is also possible that the people of Israel wanted security without moral and spiritual responsibility. The following observation is interesting at this point:

> So then, the people claimed and exercised what in these days is called "the right of self-determination." The change-over from theocracy to monarchy was of themselves. God gave them a

king and constituted a kingship. The fact would seem to be that Israel had wearied of a theocratic form of government which made their well-being dependent on their right conduct. Perhaps they vaguely supposed that a government under a human king would relieve them somewhat of this responsibility, inasmuch as their well-being would rest more with the character of the government and the qualities of the king himself.[30]

The request of the elders was a blow to Samuel. He regarded this as a personal rejection. When Samuel appeared before the Lord, he was reassured that the rejection was not of his rule, but of divine rule (v. 7). Following this prayer to the Lord, Samuel returned to the people with the instructions to "protest" their intentions and to warn them of the problems of monarchial rule (v. 9).

II. THE PRICE OF KINGSHIP (8:11-22)

Liberal scholarship usually attributes this portion of Scripture to late sources (Deuteronomic) and argues that it represents strong anti-monarchial attitudes of a much later period than the days of Saul and David.[31]

The warnings issued by Samuel were not merely the idle ramblings of a disappointed prophet, but they accurately reflected some of the more serious problems related to monarchial rule as known to us from the ancient Near East at that time. A great deal of light has been shed on Samuel's protest of kingship from the documents of Alalakh and Ugarit.[32] In the context of verses 11 through 18, five serious problems are cited by Samuel. They are as follows: (1) A military draft would be established (vv. 11-12). (2) The people of the land would be put in servitude (v. 13). (3) There would be widespread land confiscation (v.

---

[30]J. Sidlow Baxter, "Judges to Esther," *Explore the Book* (Grand Rapids: Zondervan Publishing House, 1960), II, p. 55.

[31]See E. J. Young, *My Servants the Prophets* (Grand Rapids: William B. Eerdmans Publishing Co., 1955), p. 80.

[32]I. Mendelson, "Samuel's Denunciation of Kingship in the Light of the Akkadian Documents from Ugarit," *Bulletin of the American Schools of Oriental Research,* No. 143 (Oct., 1956), p. 17.

14). Such land confiscation was common among kings of the ancient Near East. These lands were many times given to successful warriors for their own private use. (4) There would be taxes (v. 15). (5) There would be the loss of personal liberty (vv. 16-17). Samuel warned the people that whatever success might be achieved by the appointment of a king at this point would be purely temporary, and the day would come when the people would cry out for freedom from such rule (v. 18).

The warnings of Samuel went completely unheeded, however. The people at this point were not interested in the facts of monarchial rule, for their minds were made up, and again they repeated their demand to establish a king over them (v. 19). The cry of the Hebrew nation at this stage of their history is interesting. Note that two principal crisis points in Jewish history revolve around the establishment and the rejection of a king. Here the voices of Israel demand a king, but at Calvary Israel rejected their king. Observe the words of John 19:15, "We have no king." The people persisted in their demands, desiring political compatibility and jurisprudence which would be similar to that of their neighbors. They also wanted a warrior who would lead them against the encroachments of the Ammonites to the east (v. 20; cf. 12:12). Samuel was commanded to listen to the voice of the people and to give them a king (v. 22).

While it might appear at this point that the purposes of God were not being completely fulfilled, let it be noted that God in His sovereignty takes into account even the evil deeds of men and these accomplish His will (cf. the treatment of Joseph, Gen. 50:20). Israel, in its moment of wrath and sin, was, in effect, accomplishing God's purpose from the beginning — the preparation of a kingdom for His Son (Gen. 49:10; Num. 24:17).[33] Even the selection of Saul accomplished the purposes of God, for through his evil David was selected. The rule of Saul, by the very nature of the case, had to be temporary in the light of Genesis 49:10, for there the writer tells us that the scepter belonged in Judah. Therefore, even if Saul had accomplished good, his rule would have to come to an end in the light of God's prophetic plan for His Son's kingdom.

---

[33]In this connection see Ps. 76:10.

The truths of this passage call our attention to some important theological dimensions; namely, the sovereignty of God. This doctrine is often neglected and in our day the character of God is generally humanized by liberal scholarship to the point that He has no transcendent meaning to the believer. The only ultimate hope that the believer has is the fact that God is sovereign and that all things are under His control — even the evil deeds of men. As noted above, Joseph recognized this truth and was comforted by it (Gen. 50:20). This was an important element in Moses' teaching as well (cf. Exod. 7:3-5; also Rom. 9: 17). The rise and fall of kings and nations is not outside the scope of God's sovereign plan as indicated in Daniel 4:25-37.

III. THE PRIVATE APPOINTMENT OF SAUL (9:1–10:16)

Saul was the son of a Benjamite by the name of Kish and described as a "man of wealth" (Heb. *gibbôr hāyil* — cf. Ruth 2:1; II Kings 15:20). Saul possessed a number of qualities which would have commended him as a military leader. In verse 2 he is described as a "choice young man" (Heb. *bāhûr*). This expression refers to a man in the prime of life. He is also described as "goodly" (Heb. *tob*). This term ". . . describes Saul's stature, not his looks as is evident from the second half of the verse."[34]

While looking for his father's lost animals, Saul came in contact with Samuel (9:3ff.). Samuel is described in a significant manner in verses 6 and 9. He is called a "man of God" (cf. Deut. 33:1; II Kings 4:9). He is also presented as an "honorable man" whose predictions always came to pass. This latter characteristic was essential for a prophet in the light of Deuteronomy 13 and 18:22. The expressions found in verse 9 have produced a wide variety of opinions among scholars as to their precise meaning. Samuel is referred to as a "prophet" (Heb. *nābî*), whereas the earlier term was "seer" (Heb. *rō 'eh*). Some have attempted to argue for clear distinctions between these two terms, often concluding that they represented two entirely different functions

---

34S. Goldman, "Samuel," *Soncino Books of the Bible* (London: Soncino Press, 1951), p. 45.

or offices. This view has been generally rejected or modified by conservative writers.[35]

When Saul met Samuel he was informed that he would be king over Israel. Saul's immediate response was that of surprise and bewilderment, for he came from the smallest of the tribes of Israel (9:21). After a time of conversation and eating, Samuel sent the servants of Saul away and privately anointed him a "captain" (Heb. *nāgîd*) over Israel (cf. 9:22–10:1). From the standpoint of physical strength and mental capacity, Saul appears to have been a good choice. He was striking in appearance, had initiative, was brave and patriotic. Like Moses[36] and Gideon,[37] Saul was given signs to confirm the will of God in this matter. The first was an encounter with two men who would reveal the presence of the lost animals of his father (10:2). The second sign would be when he encountered men going to Bethel carrying three kids, three loaves of bread, and a bottle of wine (10:3-4). The final sign would be in Saul's meeting a company of prophets coming down from a high place singing prophetic messages (10:5ff.). Samuel promised that when he encountered the prophets the Spirit of the Lord would come upon him and he would "be turned into another man" (10:6). He was also commanded to wait for Samuel at Gilgal for a period of seven days which, as will be noted later, he failed to do. When he left Samuel, the Scripture indicates that "God gave him another heart" (10:9). This expression should not be regarded as the act of regeneration, but rather a work of the Spirit of God by which he was prepared for kingship. Regarding this change E. J. Young notes the following:

> It would, however, be a change of degree rather than of kind. Saul was to become a different man, in that he would now have the ability to act as a king should act. He would have a

---

[35]Helpful discussions of this problem can be found in E. J. Young, *op. cit.*, pp. 61-66, Hobart E. Freeman, *An Introduction to the Old Testament Prophets* (Chicago: Moody Press, 1968), p. 40 and James Smith, "The Life and Thought of the Pre-Literary Prophets," *The Seminary Review*, XIII, 4 (Summer, 1967), p. 94.

[36]Exod. 4:3-9.

[37]Judg. 6:36-39.

wider vision of the duties that were required of a king, and he would receive the capacity to carry out those duties.[38]

When the Spirit of God did descend upon him (perhaps in the same manner that He came upon the earlier judges), he took the part of a prophet and became as one of the those who came down from the high place (10:10).[39]

IV. THE PUBLIC APPOINTMENT OF SAUL (10:17-27)

Appropriately, Samuel called all the people of Israel together at Mizpeh, the location of a previous revival (cf. I Sam. 7:5-8). On this occasion Samuel again warned the people with regard to their spiritual attitude which, in effect, involved a rejection of God (v. 19). He required that the people present themselves by their tribes and by their "thousands" (Heb. 'alpîm — families). Lots were evidently used on this occasion officially to select Saul. This is indicated by the verb "taken" in verse 20. The procedure followed here was probably similar to the one Joshua followed in the case of Achan's sin (cf. Josh. 7:16-18). The king was then brought before the people and declared their leader. His appointment was accepted (v. 24). These matters were recorded in writing (v. 25). Saul's troubles, however, had already begun, for at this time an opposition party was formed consisting mainly of the "sons of Belial" (Heb. benê belîya 'al — v. 27; cf. I Sam. 1:16; 2:12).

V. CONFIRMATION OF SAUL'S KINGSHIP (11:1—12:25)

The Ammonites, decendants of Lot (Gen. 19:38), continued their belligerency toward the tribes settled in the eastern territories of Israel. It was the Ammonite military threat under the leadership of Nahash, among other things, that caused Israel to demand a king (cf. I Sam. 12:12). Nahash gave the people of Jabesh-gilead seven days to agree to his terms of surrender

---

[38]*Op. cit.*, p. 87.
[39]Cf. Judg. 3:10; 6:34; 11:29; 14:6, 19; 15:14. Also see E. J. Young, *op. cit.*, p 87 ff.

which involved the thrusting out of the right eye of the inhabitants of that city (11:2-3). The savagery of these peoples is elsewhere seen in Amos 1:13. The loss of the right eye had military implications, for it would disable the men of that city for military duty since the left eye was usually covered by the shield in battle and the right eye used to spot the enemy. This practice has also been attested in Ugaritic literature. Cyrus Gordon observes the following:

> As an illustration we may note, in both the Bible and Ugaritic literature, the idea of punishing or humiliating a city by blind-. ing its inhabitants in one eye. This barbaric usage, which is what Saul saved the people of Jabesh-gilead from (I Sam. 11:2), is now attested in Ugaritic (AQHT: 65-168). . . .[40]

The Ammonites were evidently sure of victory as evidenced by the nature of their proposal. The elders of Jabesh-gilead asked for a seven-day delay in order to formulate an official reply. Nahash responded affirmatively to this request. This concession illustrated the contemptuous regard which he had for the fighting strength of Israel.

Messengers were immediately sent from Jabesh-gilead to Saul's headquarters located at Gibeah (11:4). This site has been identified with Tell el-Ful, located just north of Jerusalem. Tell el-Ful has been excavated and has provided interesting insights into the nature of Saul's headquarters. William F. Albright, who first excavated the site, describes Saul's Gibeah as follows:

> Though strongly constructed, the fortress walls were built of hammer-dressed masonry, and its contents were extremely simple. It is probable that the fortress was originally constructed by the Philistines as one of a chain (I Sam. 10:5) and was adapted by Saul for his own purpose.[41]

---

[40]*Ugaritic Literature* (Rome: Pontifical Bible Institute, 1949), p. 5. Also see his *World of the Old Testament* (London: Phoenix House, 1960), p. 158.

[41]*The Biblical Period from Abraham to Ezra* (New York: Harper & Row Publishers, 1949), p. 50. Cf. Also Lawrence A. Sinclair "An Archaeological Study of Gibeah (Tell el-Ful)," *The Biblical Archaeologist*, XXVII, 2 (May, 1964), pp. 52-64.

Tell el-Ful (Gibeah of Saul, I Sam. 11:4; 15:34) the location of the fortress of Saul. Levant Photo Service

It is also enlightening to observe that Saul was, at this time, back in the field working as a farmer (11:5). The question has been rightly asked, "Why was he working with oxen rather than assuming the duties of a king?" Two answers have been given to this question: (1) Some feel that he returned to his former occupation until a special occasion should arise that would call him to higher responsibility. (2) Others argue that since his selection had been opposed by some (10:27), he decided to refrain from exercising monarchial rights until such opposition should subside. Either of these views is a legitimate possiblity, or perhaps both are true.

Saul's anger was aroused not only because of the bodily mutilation threatened against the inhabitants of Jabesh-gilead, but more specifically, he may have had a special concern for Benjamites living in the city. It should be remembered that in the tragic Benjamite war (Judg. 20–21) 400 women from Jabesh-gilead were given in marriage to the only surviving Benjamites

of that conflict (Judg. 21:8-12). In all probability, many of the
Benjamites returned with the women to Jabesh-gilead after their
marriage. If this were the case, then Saul's concern for the defense of the city had tribal implications. The first things Saul did
in preparation for war was to take a census to determine the
military capacity of the nation. Verse 8 indicates that a political
distinction had already arisen between Israel and Judah. Perhaps it was men from Judah who opposed the original appointment of Saul as king (10:27). This distinction is noted two other
times in the book of I Samuel (15:4; 17:52). The messengers
returned with a firm commitment of defense from Saul, which
certainly must have brought great relief to that city. The elders
of Jabesh-gilead contacted Nahash and indicated that the answer
he sought would be delivered the next day (11:10). This, of
course, was an effective delaying tactic which would lull Nahash
into a false sense of security and provide Saul and his men ade-
quate time to reach the site. Saul used this time wisely to organize his forces into three companies, perhaps following the same
procedures used by Gideon at an earlier time (cf. Judg. 7:16).
The attack came in the morning watch which was the last of
three watches (cf. Lam. 2:19; Judg. 7:19; Exod. 14:24-27). After
a complete victory, the people of Israel reaffirmed their commitment to their king at Gilgal (11:13-15).

The confirmation ceremonies at Gilgal were concluded by a
message from Samuel. The first twelve verses of Chapter 12 are
a review of the history of this period and Samuel's ministry
among the people. Samuel wanted to establish his innocence and
his fidelity to the people, but in so doing indirectly admitted
that his sons were failures (12:2-5).

The judges listed in verse 11 present special difficulties. Jerubbaal is, of course, identified with Gideon (Judg. 6:25-32). The
name "Bedan" is problematic because this name does not appear
in the book of Judges. It has been supposed by some that this is
a reference to a lesser judge whose deeds were not officially recorded. This view, however, appears to be unlikely in view of
the nature of Samuel's argument. The others listed are rather
imposing personalities connected with specific and important
events. What purpose would the name of an unknown judge
serve in his argument? Perhaps the best explanation for the ap-

pearance of this name is that it represents a copyist's error in the text for the name Barak. The Syriac, Septuagint and Arabic versions have all adopted the latter name.

The remaining section of Chapter 12 (vv. 13-25) is a severe warning to Israel with regard to their faithfulness to the Lord. If Israel and her king were obedient to Jehovah, there would be blessing and prosperity (vv. 14-15). If, however, they forsook the Lord, judgment would fall. A special sign was given to confirm the validity of this message. Thunder and rain came during the time of the wheat harvest, which was most unusual since the wheat harvest came about the end of May and early June, long after the latter rain. Again one is reminded of the spiritual depth of Samuel's ministry. His achievements were not due to mere human ingenuity, but to a sincere and consistent prayer life. This fact was clearly recognized by the people (cf. v. 19). Samuel's view of prayer and its importance in the life of the people is most instructive (v. 23; cf. 7:5; 8:6). He did not consider prayer an option to be exercised at convenient moments, but essential to an effective prophetic ministry. One wonders whether the lack of power and impact, so evident in many pulpits, is not due to the absence of fervent, continuous prayer as exemplified in the life of Samuel (and in the life of our Lord).

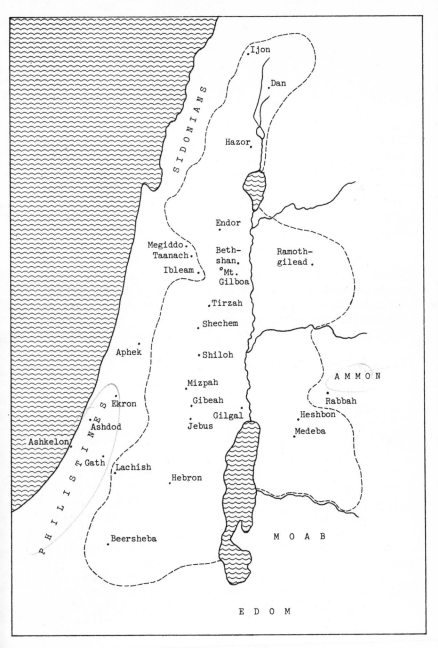

The Kingdom of Saul

Chapter 4

SAUL: A REJECTED KING

(I Samuel 13–15)

With Saul's decisive victory over the Ammonites in the East his popularity rose to unprecedented heights. When word of this victory reached the Philistine pentapolis, it became apparent that they would have to move quickly before the whole nation of Israel was militarily solidified and strengthened under monarchial leadership. In Chapters 13 to 15 of I Samuel, two of Saul's important campaigns are recorded, one directed against the Philistines in the west and the other against the Amalekites to the south. While both of these efforts produced victories, there were also some very serious discouragements because of some of Saul's personal deeds. It is entirely possible that the Ammonite victory gave Saul a false sense of self-sufficiency, for at least on two occasions he made decisions without consulting the Lord. Both cases resulted in divine rejection and judgment.

I. THE PHILISTINE WAR (13:1–14:52)

A. *Saul's Presumptuous Act at Gilgal* (13:1-23)

1. *Jonathan's Victory at Geba* (13:1-7)

The initial verse of this chapter presents a serious textual problem. A literal translation of the text would be "the son of (one) year was Saul when he began to reign and he reigned two years over Israel." It is obvious that both statements in this verse are impossible. He could not reign when he was one year old, and it is not possible to fit all the events of Saul's life into two years. Early editions of the Septuagint avoided the difficulty by omitting the verse entirely. The Syriac rendered the verse ". . . when Saul had reigned one or two years. . . ." The Targums paraphrased the verse to read "Saul was as innocent as a one year old child when he began to reign." Modern commentaries are generally agreed that the present form of the Hebrew text suffers from an omission of numbers that were originally there. The verse apparently contains two omissions and should read as follows: "Saul was . . . years old when he began to reign, and he ruled . . . and two years over Israel."[42]

Saul, at this time, was organizing a series of defenses in the central hill country. It does not appear that he intended to confront the Philistines in full force at this particular time. He had mobilized only 3,000 troops according to verse 2. The remaining elements of the army had returned to their homes. Jonathan, however, felt that the time to strike was now, before the Philistines could establish themselves in the hill country. Jonathan, therefore, struck at the Philistine garrison in Geba. The bravery and aggressiveness of Jonathan on this occasion inspired Saul and others of the Hebrew warriors. Saul then marshaled additional troops and attempted to rally the forces at Gilgal. The fact that Saul chose Gilgal as a rallying point probably indicates that large sections of the hill country were under Philistine control. That the Philistines had a very low regard for Israel is indicated by the expression, "Israel also was had in abomination" (v. 4). This is better translated from the original, "and that Israel made himself odious with the Philistines." The verb used here is the same one used in Exodus 16:20, 24 to describe manna that had been left overnight.

The staging area selected by the Philistines was the site of Michmash (v. 5). It is extremely doubtful, however, that the total number of chariots employed on this occasion numbered 30,000 as the text presently reads. The town of Michmash was located in the hill country of central Palestine, which would render such a large chariot force useless. In addition to this, the number is many times in excess of other records of chariot divisions in a single encounter. Pharaoh, for example, had only 600 chariots when he pursued the Israelites (Exod. 14:7); Sisera, 900 (Judg. 4:13); and Zera, the Ethiopian, 300 (II Chron. 14:9). In the great battle of Qarqar (853 B.C.), the coalition that met Shalmaneser III only had about 4,000 chariots.[43]

When word regarding the size of the chariot force reached the Israelites at Gilgal, many of them fled across the Jordan to the

---

[42]See John J. Davis, *Biblical Numerology*, p. 86.

[43]*Ibid.*, p. 84. Note that the number 30,000 is reduced to 3,000 in the Lucian edition of the LXX text and the Syriac.

Gorge at Michmash (I Sam. 14:4-14). Matson Photo Service

hills of Moab (v. 7). Saul at this point found himself in a most difficult position. Not only were the Philistines well equipped and prepared for a major engagement in the central hill country, but the people of Israel were badly scattered and afraid (v. 6). It was in this context that Saul took a most disastrous step in disobeying a specific command of Samuel.

2. *Saul's Disobedience and Rejection* (13:8-23)

Rather than waiting for Samuel, as previously instructed (10: 8), Saul took it upon himself to offer a burnt offering in an attempt to unify the people and perhaps to seek God's will. We do not know why Samuel was late in arriving at Gilgal, unless perhaps to test Saul's faith. In any event, when Samuel did arrive, the actions of Saul were openly challenged and rebuked by Samuel. There has been considerable discussion as to the nature of Samuel's rebuke. Was it only because Saul offered a sacrifice? This is doubtful because Solomon later offered sacrifices and apparently without rebuke (I Kings 3:4, 15). It seems that Samuel's rebuke was directed at Saul's impatience and his disobedience in not waiting for prophetic guidance. In an attempt to justify himself, Saul offered three excuses for his action. These are recorded in verse 11. They are as follows: (1) "the people were scattered," (2) "thou camest not within the days appointed," and (3) "the Philistines gathered themselves together at Michmash." Notice that Saul did not claim that he misunderstood the instructions previously given to him. They were quite clear. His disobedience was in impetuously moving ahead without prophetic counsel. Samuel did not accept the proposition that the end justified the means, and regarded Saul's actions as being foolish (v. 13). As a result of this act the Lord promised that the kingdom of Saul would not continue and the Lord would seek another man who would be more sensitive to His will (v. 14). Following the prophetic rebuke, Saul found himself with only 600 men (v. 15).

The remaining part of Chapter 13 describes the tremendous power the Philistines exercised over Israel during this period of time. Not only did the Philistines have an impressive chariot force, but also maintained their monopoly over the use of iron

(v. 19). This monopoly continued with some success until the time of David when Israel began to produce iron objects rather freely (cf. I Chron. 22:3). The reading of verse 21 is made very difficult in the Authorized Version because the translators did not understand the Hebrew text. The phrase translated "yet they had a file" is now better translated "and the price was a pim" or "the charge was a pim." In recent years small weights have been discovered at Lachish, Jerusalem, Gezer and Tell En-Nasbeh with the Hebrew letters *pim* inscribed on them. The *pim* weight represented two-thirds of a shekel. The actual weight was about one-quarter of an ounce.

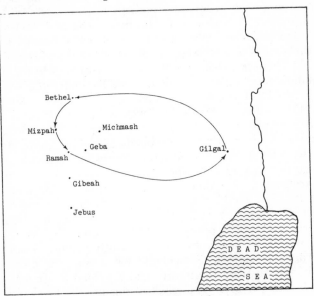

The Cities of Samuel

B. *The Battle of Michmash* (14:1-23)

The major battle took place at the town of Michmash (v. 5). The account of the battle is an exciting one and gives significant insight into the character and heroism of Jonathan, as well as providing extremely accurate topographical information concerning that area. Note, for example, Jonathan's confidence as expressed in verse 6, "It may be that the Lord will work for us for there is no restraint to the Lord to save by many or by few." Jonathan was perhaps recalling the historical events surrounding Gideon's defeat of the Midianites (Judg. 7:4 ff.). By means of a careful strategy and a great earthquake provided by God (vv. 15, 20, 23) a crucial victory was achieved in this initial engagement. The nation was badly depressed and scattered. This heroic act on Jonathan's part provided the inspired leadership necessary to rally the forces again. Hebrews who had hidden themselves in caves were now prepared to join the battle in pursuit of the Philistines westward to Beth-aven (v. 23). Many of the Hebrews were fighting as allies with the Philistines at this time (v. 21). Some scholars feel that these individuals were probably slaves captured from Israel in previous raids; however, it seems more likely that they were professional soldiers or mercenaries who had sold themselves into military service. When the Israelites were victorious, they changed their allegiance and fought with Saul.

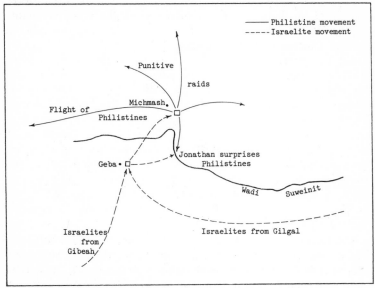

The Battle of Michmash

C. *A Rash Oath* (14:24-45)

Rather than immediately pursuing the enemy to complete the
defeat of their forces, as one would expect, Saul took this occasion to exercise his authority, evidently for its own sake. He pro-
claimed a decree that no one was to eat food until the evening
in order that "I may be avenged of mine enemies" (v. 24). It is
obvious from Saul's statement that he had lost true perspective of
the situation. This was not his war, nor were they particularly
"his" enemies; they were the Lord's (v. 23). There may be a
number of reasons why Saul issued the decree at this time. Perhaps he was trying to reinstate himself in the eyes of the people,
having been humbled by the previous rebuke at the hands of
Samuel. It is also likely that he feared the growing popularity
of Jonathan, who at this point was regarded as a military hero.
The people, however, were not in a position effectively to maintain a continuous pursuit because "they were faint" (v. 28).
Jonathan obviously disagreed with this decree and its implications (v. 29). He knew that this would destroy the strength and
morale of the Israelite army which was on the verge of victory.
As the Israelite armies marched westward down to the valley of
Ajalon, a distance of some twenty miles from Michmash, they became extremely hungry and were very weak (v. 31). When
they came upon the spoil of the enemy, they took of the cattle
and sheep, slew them, and ate the meat with the blood (v. 32).
This, of course, was in direct violation of the law of Leviticus
19:26. Saul had not only weakened the fighting potential of Israel with his rash oath, but he had also caused the people to sin.
Recognizing the seriousness of this situation with respect to possible immediate divine punishment, he commanded that a large
stone be brought to him in order that the animals could be slain
on it, thus allowing the blood to run off. Shortly after this Saul
erected an altar in an attempt to acquire divine counsel, but
without avail (v. 37).

Jonathan, not knowing of his father's decree (v. 27), had eaten
some honey. Saul became violently angry when word reached
him that his decree had been publicly violated. He demanded
the death of Jonathan his son (vv. 39-44). The people, however,
would not permit this to happen and went to the aid of Jonathan

(v. 45). Could it be that the political honeymoon was coming to an end?

D. *Summary of Saul's Reign* (14:46-52)

The verse which concludes this chapter represents a summary of Saul's military activity. During his reign he fought the enemies on every side and secured the central hill country and much of the steppe lands for Israel, although most of his battles were defensive in nature. The principal enemy throughout his reign was Philistia according to verse 52. While Saul enjoyed some limited success in battle against them, they were still a serious threat at the end of Saul's reign.

II. THE AMALEKITE WAR (15:1-35)

South of Israel in the Negeb, large areas were occupied by a people well known for their vicious fighting ability. Shortly after Israel's exodus from Egypt it was the Amalekites who attempted to prevent Israel from moving into the Sinai Peninsula (cf. Exod. 17). The Lord had not forgotten that encounter and it was promised on that occasion that Amalek and his descendants would be utterly destroyed (Exod. 17:14). When Joshua entered Canaan, the Amalekites were either not near the areas defeated by Joshua or he consciously avoided contact with them, for we do not read of any major confrontation with these peoples. In any event, by this time they had grown to considerable size and had developed an impressive fighting force. Judah and Simeon, therefore, must have been under constant threat from these peoples. In view of this situation and previous history, God, through Samuel, commanded their total destruction (Heb. *ḥerem*). Such a command was not an encouragement to the barbaric slaughter of "innocent people" as some have argued, but represents a fully justified act on the part of a holy God who reserves the right to judge sin at any point in history (cf. v. 18). So Sodom and Gomorrah fell under God's judgment (Gen. 19), as did Jericho (Josh. 6) and Ai (Josh. 8). Destructions of this kind were not based on mere political or military considerations, but especially on religious (cf. Deut. 7:2-6; 12:2-3; 20:10-18). Furthermore, the fact that this command came from God, it, *a priori*, is just, by virtue of the perfect character of God. For a full discussion of the application of the *ḥerem* principle in the Old Testament, see the book *Conquest and Crisis*.[44]

Since this battle was to be fought in the open spaces of the desert, Saul used an army of much larger proportion than previously employed in the hill country (v. 4). The initial encounter with the enemy resulted in victory for Saul and his forces. However, Saul made the fatal mistake of not completely obeying the instruction of Samuel in applying the total "ban" (Heb. *ḥerem*) upon the people. Allowing King Agag to live was clearly in violation of God's original command. In all probability others were permitted to live as well, for it was not many years later that they attacked and destroyed Ziklag, the residence of David (I Sam. 30). Animals belonging to the Amalekites were also kept alive as booty, presumably to be used for sacrifices (v. 21). This disobedience on the part of Saul brought "repentance" to the heart of Jehovah (vv. 11, 35). The "repentance" of God should not be regarded as remorse because of an error in judgment, but deep sorrow in the light of man's failure in spite of divine provision (cf. Gen. 6:6). God's laws and decrees do not change (cf. 15:29); but as men change, different laws operate.

The next morning Samuel paid a visit to Saul to discuss the results of the campaign. As he approached Gilgal, he was greeted by Saul who very proudly said, "I have performed the commandment of the Lord" (v. 13). Note the emphasis on the pronoun "I." But Samuel raised a rather embarrassing question, for he heard the sound of many sheep and other animals which had been brought back from the battle. The shift in pronouns on the part of Saul is interesting. Saul replied to Samuel's penetrating question by saying, "*They* have brought them from the Amalekites" (v. 15). He concluded his response asserting ". . . the rest *we* have utterly destroyed" (v. 15). The shift in pronouns is an obvious example of the ancient (and modern) art of "passing the buck." Saul attempted to justify the deeds of the people on the grounds that their intentions were good. In other words, the end had fully justified the means. He assumed that any sacri-

---

44John J. Davis, pp. 48-49.

fice, whether prepared in disobedience or obedience, would be acceptable to God. How far he had missed the point! The rebuke of Samuel for this philosophy was quick and decisive. Samuel rightly observed that the Lord delighted more in genuine obedience than the mere slaughter of an animal (even though that was important too, cf. v. 22). The response of Samuel should not be interpreted as an "anti-priestly polemic" as some have asserted. Samuel was merely pointing out a basic truth that sacrifices *in themselves* were not the final answer to man's need in restoring fellowship with his God. A true sacrifice was to be a genuine sign of faith and obedience. If sacrifices were offered in apostasy and unbelief, they were as worthless as the sacrifices of the Canaanites in the sight of a holy God (cf. Isa. 1:11; 66:3; Jer. 6:20; Hos. 6:6; and Mic. 6:6-8). Following the rebuke of Samuel, Saul confessed his sin (v. 24). One wonders how genuine this confession really was (cf. the words of Pharaoh, Exod. 9:27). The result of this disobedience on the part of Saul led to his final rejection as king of Israel (vv. 23, 26).

In the presence of Saul and the soldiers, Agag, king of the defeated Amalekites, was put to death by Samuel (v. 33). Samuel then returned to his home in Ramah, and Saul went to Gibeah in Benjamin. The sin of Saul not only led to rejection and separation with respect to God, but with Samuel as well (v. 35).

What tremendous changes had taken place in the monarchial situation of Israel and in the life of Saul. Saul had all the qualities of greatness, but his independent spirit and pride had stripped him of the glory that could have been his. His early career was characterized by initiative and aggressiveness which resulted in victories (cf. 11:7), but this later degenerated into mere personal ambition (20:31). What was originally outstanding bravery (13:3) turned into a form of recklessness (14:24). Like Samson, he was a man of talent and ability, but these were only an asset to his leadership as they were committed to God and brought into conformity to His will.

The experiences of Saul are an unmistakable lesson to believers of all ages. The possession of physical attractiveness, talent and popularity does not guarantee divine blessing or success in one's pursuits.

Chapter 5

A VALIANT SHEPHERD
(I Samuel 16–20)

Following divine rejection of Saul's kingship, and the personal separation of Samuel from Saul, the Biblical narrative now shifts its emphasis from Saul to David. The utter failure of Saul and his gross disobedience to God's will led to heartbreak on the part of Samuel. As Samuel sat in his hometown, Ramah, and contemplated the political future of Israel, he probably saw nothing but ominous clouds of despair and confusion. This led him to great searching of soul and mourning (16:1). That situation was about to be changed, however. The silence of the heavens was broken, and Samuel was commanded to cease his mourning and move ahead in pursuit of new prospects and new opportunities for the deliverance of Israel.

I. DAVID CHOSEN AND ANOINTED (16:1-13)

A. *Samuel's Journey to Bethlehem* (16:1-11)

Samuel was commanded to fill his horn with oil and prepare to go to Bethlehem to anoint the new king of Israel. This request, however, brought fear to Samuel, for he calculated that if Saul should hear of such a deed, his life would be brought to an end (v. 2). The Lord cared for this situation by requiring that he take a heifer with him for the purpose of sacrifice to Jehovah. It was not in the best public interest at this time to conduct a public anointing of David. It must always be remembered that the will of God has three dimensions: the man, the place, and the time. When all these factors are brought together in conformity to God's will, there is success and accomplishment. Samuel, as he had done in the past, obeyed the Lord even though it meant jeopardizing his own life. When he arrived in Bethlehem, the elders of the town were greatly afraid at his presence. Perhaps they expected the pronouncement of judgment, or perhaps the presence of the prophet at this time of the year was most unusual

(v. 4). In any event, they were assured that his presence there was for peaceful reasons. They were commanded to "sanctify themselves" in preparation for the sacrifice (v. 5). The sanctification referred to here was basically ceremonial, relating to the washings and legal purifications which accompanied a sacrifice (cf. Exod. 19:10, 14, 22).

When Jesse and his sons came to Samuel, Samuel was instructed not to regard their outward appearance in considering the next king, but the total man. The Israelites had already made the mistake of selecting a king on the basis of physical qualities alone. Samuel was reminded that the Lord looks on the heart while man looks on the physical appearance (v. 7). The original text of this verse is very expressive. It literally reads, "Man sees the eyes, but Jehovah sees the heart." The Hebrew term *'ênayim* ("eyes") refers to the visible outward appearance of man, the physical qualities, while the Hebrew term *lēḇāḇ* ("heart") refers to the innermost spiritual and psychological qualities of man. It was natural for Jesse to expect the eldest of the sons to be selected, but as is the case with God's elective plan, many times the younger is selected above the elder (cf. Rom. 9:11-13). When David appeared before Samuel, it was clear that he was God's choice. David is described as being "ruddy" (Heb. *'aḏmônî* — "reddish"). This expression is usually considered to refer to the color of his hair ". . . which was regarded as a mark of beauty in southern lands, where the hair is generally black."[45] The other expressions in this verse lead us to believe that David was a very attractive young man. At the Lord's command, Samuel took the oil and anointed him in the presence of his brothers and his father. On this occasion, the Spirit of the Lord came upon David (as He came upon the judges before him), thus enabling him to fulfill the specific tasks which God assigned to him (cf. I Sam. 10:6, 10). This anointing was the first of three anointings. The second was when he was made king over Judah at Hebron (II Sam. 2:4), and the third when he was chosen king over all the nation of Israel (II Sam. 5:3).

---

[45]C. F. Keil and F. Delitzsch, *op. cit.*, p. 169, also S. Goldman, *op. cit.*, p. 95.

II. A MEETING WITH THE KING (16:14-23)

A. *The Departure of the Spirit* (16:14)

When the Spirit came upon David in the anointing ceremony, the Spirit of God departed from Saul; that is, the gifts for kingship were taken from Saul. The difficulty in verse 14 is the interpretation of the last clause which says, ". . . an evil spirit from the Lord troubled him."

1. *The Nature of This Event*

There are various viewpoints as to the meaning of the expression "evil spirit from the Lord" and what precisely happened when the spirit "troubled him." The following are some representative views: (a) Saul was demon possessed. The following discussion is perhaps most representative of this viewpoint:

> The "evil spirit from Jehovah" which came into Saul in the place of the Spirit of Jehovah, was not merely an inward feeling of depression at the rejection announced to him, which grew into melancholy, and occasionally broke out in passing fits of insanity, but a higher evil power, which took possession of him, and not only deprived him of his peace of mind, but stirred up the feelings, ideas, imagination, and thoughts of his soul to such an extent that at times it drove him even into madness. This demon is called "an evil spirit (coming) from Jehovah" because Jehovah sent it as a punishment. . . .[46]

(b) Some have suggested that this evil spirit was an evil messenger, perhaps analogous to the situation in I Kings 22:20-23. (c) The evil spirit was, in effect, "a spirit of discontent" created by God in the heart of Saul. This view draws on the analogy of Judges 9:23 where it is stated that God "sent an evil spirit between Abimelech and the men of Shechem. . . ."

2. *The Effects of This Event*

Most commentators who hold the above views are agreed that the effects of the evil spirit working in Saul's life were mental and psychological.

---

[46]C. F. Keil and F. Delitzsch, *op. cit.*, p. 170.

> Saul is afflicted by a form of insanity which manifested itself in sudden fits of terror, unreasoning rages and on occasions homicidal violence. The symptoms suggest manic depressive psychosis.[47]

The ancient historian Josephus describes the situation as follows:

> But as for Saul, some strange and demonical disorders came upon him, and brought upon him such suffocations as were ready to choke him. . . .[48]

Whatever this malady was, it was a serious one which brought great concern to Saul's servants. They recognized that a solution to the problem was the playing of music (v. 16). When this evil spirit was upon him, he evidently went into a frenzied condition in which he lost control of his emotions and his actions (cf. 18:1-11). When David played upon the lyre, this returned Saul to psychological normalcy (cf. v. 23 — Heb. *rāwaḥ lešā'ûl* — "Saul's spirit revived"; "Saul was refreshed"). When a man was sought out to provide the necessary music for Saul's comfort, David's name was suggested. This, of course, was no accident, and is reminiscent of the rise of Joseph in the Egyptian royal court.

B. *A Perspective on David* (16:18-23)

There can be no doubt in one's mind as to the attractiveness of David. He was a man of many skills which included the playing of an instrument as well as courage in times of danger. The expressions, "mighty valiant man," and "a man of war" (v. 18), need not refer to military combat alone, but also to his conflicts with lions and bears (cf. 17:34-35). Perhaps the outstanding quality of David was the fact that "the Lord was with him" (v. 18). Even at this point in his career, this fact must have been evident to those associated with him. David's skill and his graciousness endeared him to Saul (v. 21).

---

[47]S. Goldman, *op. cit.*, p. 96.
[48]*Antiquities* VI.8.2 (Hereafter referred to as *Ant.*)

III. DAVID AND GOLIATH (17:1-58)

A. *The Philistine Challenge* (17:1-14)

The Philistines who had been badly beaten at Michmash (14:
4 ff.) had regrouped themselves for another encounter with Israel. The stage was set approximately seventeen miles southwest of Jerusalem between Shochoh and Azekah. Because of their
severe losses at Michmash and elsewhere, they decided to confront the Israelites by means of representative combat, a common practice in the ancient Near East by which one individual
would represent an army. The man chosen for this task was Goliath of Gath (v. 4). He stood about nine feet, six inches, tall.
Many feel that he was a descendant of the gigantic sons of Anak,
who, according to Joshua 11:22, were still resident in the southwest corner of Palestine. The details regarding the armor of Goliath are of interest. Most of his defensive equipment was made
of bronze, whereas the weapons of attack were made of iron.[49]
Not only was the armor of Goliath impressive, but his claims
were as well. He was obviously a very arrogant man, and one
who had not suffered defeat in the past. He called himself "the
Philistine" (v. 8 — Heb. *happelištî*).

B. *A Shepherd's Courage* (17:15-58)

The acts of David recorded in the remaining verses of Chapter
17 not only reflect his great courage, but also indicate that he
was a man of great faith. In the past he had been confronted by
wild beasts which, humanly speaking, would have created a situation of disaster; but because the Lord intervened in his behalf,
such was not the case (vv. 34-37). David was confident, that as
God's anointed, he would be protected.

When David was to face Goliath, he prepared for the situation
by taking five stones and his sling which he had great skill in using. The sling used in David's day consisted of two long cords
with a leather or wooden pocket fastened to them. After the

---

[49]The Hebrew word *neḥošet* should be translated "bronze" which is an
alloy of copper and tin, rather than "brass," a compound metal made of
copper and zinc. Brass was not used until a later period.

stone was placed in the pocket, the sling was whirled around the head, and one string released, thus casting the stone with terrific force. The stones used were generally rather large (two or three inches in diameter) and made from flint or limestone. Apparently the Israelites had developed considerable skill in the use of such slings (cf. Judg. 20:16). The presence of David was considered a complete insult to Goliath, and he immediately held

Shepherd Boy with Sling. Matson Photo Service

David in the highest of contempt. He asked David if he considered him to be a dog (v. 43); that is, the lowest of animal creatures in the land. The dialogue between David and Goliath is an interesting comparison of attitudes and beliefs. In a brief period of time the victory was David's. Not only was Goliath slain at the hand of this humble shepherd, but his head was cut off and kept. Verse 54 indicates that David brought the head to Jerusalem as a war trophy for all to see, but the armor of Goliath was kept for himself. This verse also presents a problem since it appears that the Jebusites were still in control of the city (II Sam. 5:6). Two explanations are possible here. One would be that the account anticipates the conquest of Jerusalem by David and the ultimate placing of the head at Jerusalem as a war trophy. The other would be that the city had been temporarily conquered by the Israelites, as was the case in the past, but was not permanently held by them (cf. Judg. 1:8, 21).

Saul's questions recorded in verses 55 through 58 create a rather difficult problem in the light of 16:18, 23 and 17:37-38. It would appear from the previous account that Saul had already been introduced to David and knew him well; however, the text at hand gives the impression that Saul did not know him and was inquiring as to his identity. Three explanations are usually offered as a solution to the problem at hand. (a) The evil spirit that came upon Saul (16:14) brought a mental malady that affected his memory. Some argue that Saul had only seen David in fits of madness and did not recognize him when sane (cf. 16: 23); however, the account of Chapter 16, verses 21 and following, implies that David was a regular member of Saul's retinue, and therefore was in his presence quite regularly, not merely to play music. (b) Some argue that a considerable length of time had elapsed since his last visit to the court, and as he was then in very early manhood, he had, so to speak, grown, in a comparatively short length of time, out of Saul's memory. However, it is doubtful that a great period of time elapsed between verses 54 and 55 of this chapter. Surely, Saul would have attempted to meet this hero as soon as possible after the defeat of the Philistines. (c) Saul was not inquiring about David, but about his father's worth and social condition in order that he might know the parentage of his future son-in-law, or for some other similar reasons.[50]

David's victory over Goliath was a turning point in his life. It not only gave to Israel renewed opportunity to strengthen themselves with respect to Philistine incursion but it, in fact, confirmed David's anointing to the kingship. David's victory over

---

[50]See C. F. Keil and F. Delitzsch, *op. cit.*, p. 186. Discussion of this problem can also be found in H. D. M. Spence, *op. cit.*, p. 369.

this giant is also an excellent example of the divine principles of operation as explained by the Apostle Paul in I Corinthians 1:27-28.

IV. LIFE IN THE ROYAL COURT (18:1–20:42)

A. *Jonathan and David* (18:1-5)

The very warm and human relationship sustained by Jonathan and David is one of the bright spots in the narratives of I Samuel. In contrast to the cold rebellion of Saul is the very warm sensitivity of his son and heir to the throne, Jonathan. The covenant of friendship established between Jonathan and David (v. 3) was something that Jonathan probably longed for, for he could not find it with his father because of his father's lack of spiritual insight. The evidence of Jonathan's genuine love for David is witnessed in verse 4. The precious gifts given to David were not only a ratification of their pact, but coming from the heir apparent to the throne, this was a public mark of honor. Further evidence of the Holy Spirit's ministry in David's life is seen in verse 5. In every assignment given to him by King Saul, David "behaved himself wisely," and as a result he was one of the military leaders in Israel.

B. *The Jealousy of Saul* (18:6–19:11)

1. *The Reasons for His Jealousy* (18:6-8)

The success of David in warfare, and his growing popularity, became a matter of great concern to Saul. To compound the problem the number one folk song of that era was "Saul has slain his thousands, but David his ten thousands" (v. 7). This song was not only well known to the Israelites, but apparently the Philistines had heard it and reflected this knowledge on two occasions (I Sam. 21:11; 29:5). There were, therefore, two fundamental reasons for Saul's deep jealousy regarding David's success. The first was the fact that David had captivated the imagination of the Israelites throughout the land, and had risen so rapidly in popularity. The folk song was quite clearly a thorn in Saul's side (v. 8). The other reason for Saul's jealousy is detected in verse

12, and that was Saul's great fear of David. It was quite evident to Saul that David was, indeed, especially blessed of God, and at the same time he was probably cognizant of the fact that the Spirit of God had departed from him, thus leaving him without the skills and abilities necessary for successful rulership.

2. *The Results of His Jealousy* (18:9 ff.)

Needless to say, one of the clear evidences of Saul's jealousy was his open hatred and anger toward David (v. 8). His deep fear of David's rise to power was also one of the products of his deep jealousy (18:12). Perhaps the other obvious result of his disposition of jealousy was the numbered attempts on David's life, the first of which is recorded in this chapter. Apparently on two occasions Saul threatened the life of David (vv. 10-11), but on both occasions David was able to escape. There is some question as to whether the javelin was thrown on both occasions or on just one. In any event, David demonstrated his graciousness and his patience in returning to the presence of Saul in spite of the obvious attempts on his life. Most of us would not have been inclined to subject ourselves to this type of treatment a second time. In the light of Saul's attempts with the javelin, something might be said by way of David's skill and maneuverability, for not only on this occasion was he able to escape, but evidently on subsequent occasions as well (cf. 19:10). One wonders what the palace wall must have looked like in view of Saul's fruitless attempts with the javelin! Where these personal attempts of taking the life of David had failed, Saul attempted more subtle means. By putting David in the forefront of Philistine confrontation, Saul hoped that his life would be taken, and in this way he would not be directly responsible for his death (cf. vv. 17, 25). Saul used his two daughters to try to accomplish this, the one named Merab, and the other, Michal. David, of course, was not aware of these subtle attempts at this time; and much to Saul's distress, David was successful in his conquest of the Philistines, thus fulfilling the requirements for receiving Michal as his wife (cf. vv. 25-28).[51]

---

[51]Is it possible that David got his plan for Uriah's death from these experiences? (cf. II Sam. 11:15.)

Jonathan became rather concerned over the growing rift between Saul and David. In an attempt to patch up a crumbling
relationship, Jonathan spoke well of David before his father and
encouraged his father not to attempt to take the life of David
(vv. 4-5). To this admonition Saul agreed and swore that David
would not be slain (v. 6). With this encouragement, David returned to the royal court of Saul, and tried to soothe the savage
soul of Saul when the evil spirit came upon him by playing his
lyre as he had done on previous occasions. While David played
the lyre, Saul sought for the third time to slay him with the javelin, and once again David was successful in fleeing this attempt.[52]
From this point onward, David became a fugitive and an out-
cast with regard to the royal court.

C. David's Escape (19:12–20:42)

After David left the royal court, he returned to his house and
to his wife, Michal, who, upon hearing of Saul's attempts on his
life, made provision for David's escape. David was let down
through a window which made possible his flight from the city
(19:12). It is entirely possible that David's house was situated
along the outer city wall, much like the location of Rahab's house
(Josh. 2:15). To help cover his escape and to gain more time,
Michal took "the image" (Heb. hatterāpîm) and placed it in the
bed (19:13). This is a rather unique usage of the term "teraphim," for this expression usually refers to rather small household
deities. In addition to the image, or "the teraphim," she put a
"quilt of goats' hair" in the bed either to cover the complete image or to give the appearance of hair on the image placed in the
bed. The translators of the Septuagint confused the Hebrew
kebîr ("quilt") with kābēd ("liver") and translated the expression as a "goat's liver." Josephus adopted this interpretation,
and in his Antiquities of the Jews suggested that a palpitating
liver was placed in the bed to give the impression of life.[53]

---

[52]Perhaps David made the mistake of playing the popular folk tune mentioned in 18:7; 21:1 and 29:5!

[53]VI.11.4. See also S. Goldman, op. cit., p. 118 and C. F. Keil and
F. Delitzsch, op. cit., p. 195.

From here David fled to Ramah, the hometown of Samuel (19: 18). Perhaps David needed counsel in these times of great distress. When Saul heard of David's presence in Ramah, he sent three contingents of messengers to attempt to take David, which attempts were rendered useless because of the ministry of the Spirit of God. On all three occasions, the Spirit came upon the messengers and they prophesied (19:20-22). In utter frustration Saul decided to go to Ramah himself and capture David, only to experience the same thing, namely, the descent of the Spirit of God causing him to prophesy and to strip off clothing in a manner that would cause others to ask, "Is Saul also among the prophets?" (19:22-24). When David heard of Saul's presence in the city, he was forced to flee once again, and this time he came to Jonathan and pled his case before his closest friend. In rather amazing words, Jonathan told David ". . . my father will do nothing" (20:2). Had Jonathan so quickly forgotten the events described in Chapter 19, or is it possible that he fully believed his father's oath recorded in 19:6? Jonathan made a valiant attempt to reconcile Saul and David for the second time. A very elaborate procedure was formulated by which Jonathan could determine the will of his father and try as best possible to influence that will in favor of David; however, it became very apparent to Jonathan that any attempt at reconciliation at this stage would be impossible. In fact, the attempt of Jonathan to reconcile the two sent his father into a rage which almost ended up in the slaying of Jonathan himself (20:33).

The stories of Saul and David recorded in these chapters are most instructive. They give insight into what happens to a man whose programs and prospects are conditioned only by his own will and interest. In contrast, David's attitudes reflect a heart which is controlled by the Spirit of God. His conduct at this point exemplifies the highest ideals of a spiritual life. He showed patience, love, discretion, and spiritual insight. These are the very qualities that bring success.

Chapter 6

THE ADVENTURES OF A FUGITIVE
(I Samuel 21—27)

Widespread popularity and permanent security were not often the lot of godly people in the Old Testament era. This was especially true with David during these tragic years of separation from the royal court. Perhaps one of the greatest frustrations experienced by David was the fact that his persecutors came from within Israel as well as without. These chapters in the book of I Samuel are most important if one is to understand properly the background and circumstances of many of the Psalms. One learns quite a bit about David the Psalmist in these chapters, as well as about David the fugitive. Out of his rich and varied experiences come some of the most eloquent expressions of praise as well as petition to his God. The highest of human joys as well as the deepest of personal sorrows are given fullest expression.

I. TRAGEDY AT NOB (21:1—22:23)

A. *A Visit to the Sanctuary* (21:1-10)

After David parted company with his friend Jonathan (20:42), he came to the town of Nob which was located between Anathoth and Jerusalem according to Isaiah 10:30, 32. This is the first reference in Scripture to this site. It is mentioned a total of six times in the entire Old Testament, four of which occur in Chapters 21 and 22. At the site of Nob, David came in contact with Ahimelech the priest. It is apparent that the tabernacle was now located at Nob rather than at Shiloh. As noted earlier, this was due to the fact that Shiloh had been destroyed by the Philistines. The Ark of the Covenant, however, was still in the house of Abinadab in Kirjath-jearim (cf. 7:2 with II Sam. 6:2-3). Ahimelech was the son of Ahitub (22:9) and therefore a great-grandson of Eli (14:3). The chart on page 35 illustrates the relationship of Ahimelech to the family of Eli. David was afraid of the strong allegiance of Ahimelech to Saul and therefore decided

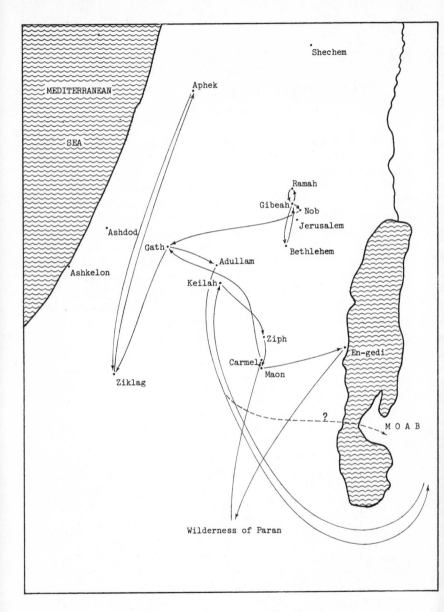

David's Wanderings (I Sam. 19—30)

that the only way to get help was to lie regarding his business in the area. He did this by deceiving Ahimelech into believing that he was there on official business from the royal court of Saul. This was the second lie told by David in a short period of time (cf. 20:6). David evidently adopted what is commonly known today as a "situational ethic." He assumed that the situation was of such a nature that the greatest good could be accomplished by getting food for his men at the cost of truth. This perhaps was the same feeling shared by Abraham in deceiving the king in Egypt (Gen. 12:13). Recall also the lies of Rahab (Josh. 2:4) and David's wife, Michal (I Sam. 19:14). The concept of a situational ethic, therefore, is not a new one. The very fact that these sins were recorded are an evidence of divine inspiration of Scripture since they involve some of the great heroes of the Old Testament. As is the case with many lies, they seem to meet the immediate need of a given situation, but have ultimate effects which perhaps were not foreseen by the one lying. Such was the case in David's experience, for this lie led to the ultimate destruction of the city (cf. 22:22 ff.).

David's need at this point was food for himself and those with him. The pitiful condition of the priesthood of this time is evidenced by the fact that there was no common bread available to them (v. 4). The only bread that Ahimelech could make available to David was the loaves kept on the table of shewbread, which bread was hallowed (v. 6). According to the law, the old bread was to be eaten by the priest and only in the holy place (Lev. 24:9); however, an exception was made in this situation. The whole transaction was not carried out in secret, and was openly witnessed by a man who would ultimately bring destruction to the city of Nob. This man is identified as Doeg, an Edomite. The question has been raised as to why an Edomite would be present at a place like this, and holding the position of "chiefest of the herdmen that belonged to Saul" (v. 7). Three views have been suggested in solving this problem. The first is that Doeg was a proselyte and therefore had won acceptance in the royal court of Saul as a religious functionary. Another view is that the term "Edomite" is used only as geographical designation and Doeg was, in effect, an Israelite who had lived in Edom.

The final suggestion is that Doeg was one of many captives brought back as a result of Saul's campaign recorded in 14:47.

Recognizing the need for armor in the light of the military pressure upon him, David requested that the sword of Goliath the Philistine be given to him. It was evidently kept in a prominent place in the tabernacle behind the ephod (v. 9). David, of course, had some claim to this since he had killed Goliath and it was with this sword that Goliath's head was cut off (17:50-51).

B. *Encounter with Achish* (21:10-15)

After David's conversation with Jonathan it became apparent that to remain in Israel at this point would be most precarious. Saul's hatred and malice had reached such an intense level that David's life and the life of his friends would be in severe danger if he remained in the reach of Saul. He fled southwest to the country of the Philistines and came to the city of Gath which was ruled by Achish. In Psalm 34, Achish is given the name Abimelech which was probably the standing title of Philistine princes at Gath. Another explanation of the two names is that the Philistine name was Achish and the Semitic form of the name was Abimelech. The journey from Nob to Gath would have been a distance of about thirty miles. It is very doubtful that Saul would think of looking for David in a Philistine city. Also, David was rather well acquainted with the countryside, for it was there he had obtained the dowry for his wife by a victory over the Philistines. In certain respects, it seems rather strange that David would go to the city of Gath, the hometown of Goliath (17:4). Perhaps he felt that he would not be recognized, for some time had elapsed since his victory over Goliath; however, if he carried the sword of Goliath with him, this certainly would have given him away. In addition to that, he must have been identified by some of the people, for they remembered the popular folk tune so well known in Israel that "Saul has slain his thousands, and David his ten thousands" (v. 11; cf. 29:5). When David saw that he had been identified, his only hope was to act out insanity, and that he did with an "Oscar winning," dramatic performance. This act must have been rather convincing, for he was released. In this very narrow escape, David was preserved for future kingship.

C. *From Adullam to Mizpeh* (22:1-5)

After escaping from the city of Gath, David went eastward into the hill country of Judah to the cave of Adullam, which, according to Josephus, was located near the city of Adullam.[54] Others feel that the cave of Adullam is located in the neighborhood of Bethlehem as implied in II Samuel 23:13-14. The cave must have been one of considerable size, for he had with him ap-

---

[54]*Ant.* VI.12.3.

View of the Judean Wilderness from the main entrance of the Cave of Adullam. It was here that David gathered to himself 400 men (I Sam. 22:1-2). Levant Photo Service

proximately 400 men (vv. 1, 2), which number would soon be
increased to 600 (cf. 23:13). Because of the unchanging belligerency of Saul, David feared for the safety of his parents. In order
to afford them protection, he went further eastward to Mizpeh
of Moab, and there placed his father and mother in the custody
of the king. Mizpeh was probably a small fortress or watchtow-
er in the mountain country. The Moabites probably viewed David as an enemy of Saul, and therefore were willing to care for
his parents, perhaps in exchange for a favor on his part. In this
hour of flight and confusion, David was approached by the
prophet Gad, who must have been a welcome sight. It is entirely possible that Samuel had sent this prophet to join David
and to give him spiritual counsel. This prophet had a long career
with David (II Sam. 24:11, 19), and along with Nathan, the
prophet, was one of the compilers of David's biography (I Chron.
29:29). The prophet's advice to David was not to remain in Mizpeh, but to return to Judah to the forest of Hareth (v. 5) which
was located northwest of Hebron on the edge of the mountain
district.

D. *The Destruction of Nob* (22:6-23)

Word came to Saul by way of his watchmen that David had
returned to the hills of Judah, but he probably did not know his
precise location. Saul called together his servants, and his standing army which evidently was made up of men from his own
tribe (chap. 7). The persecution complex from which Saul suffered was very much in evidence in his speech to the Benjamites
recorded in verse 8. Listening to that speech was Doeg, the
Edomite, who at this point saw a perfect opportunity for political advantage and further advancement. He was already "set
over the servants of Saul" (v. 9) and perhaps took this opportunity to advance himself even further in the royal court. He
informed Saul of David's encounter with Ahimelech at the city
of Nob, and the fact that Ahimelech inquired of the Lord for David, gave him food, and gave to him the sword of Goliath, the
Philistine (v. 10). Saul initiated an immediate inquiry into the
matter (v. 11). When Ahimelech appeared before the king, he
admitted to helping David but was not aware of the fact that Da-

vid was the enemy of Saul and that he was turning against the crown in giving David aid (vv. 14-15). The explanation was not satisfactory to Saul, however, and he pronounced condemnation upon Ahimelech and those who associated with him (v. 16).

Saul then called together his footmen (Heb. *rāṣîm* — "runners") and commanded them to go to the city of Nob and slay all the priests at that city as well as other inhabitants including men, women, and children (v. 19). The Hebrew term translated "footmen" in the Authorized Version is sometimes used of the royal bodyguard, which appears to be the usage here. Samuel probably had this position in mind when he warned Israel that a king would take their sons and use them "to run before his chariots" (8:11). One wonders what must have gone through the minds of these Israelite soldiers as they heard the command of Saul to slay the priests of the Lord. They normally followed all orders of Saul, but this was too much and they refused to slay the priests of the Lord. Saul did have a friend in Doeg, the Edomite, who was looking for this very opportunity to gain additional favor in the sight of the king. He followed out Saul's command and slew eighty-five priests of the city of Nob, and in addition to that, men, women, children, and animals. Evidently, Saul put the city under the ban (Heb. *ḥerem*). One young priest, Abiathar, was able to escape and he came to David. When David heard of the tragedy of Nob, he began to look back to the causes of that tragedy. He probably remembered his lie, and now viewed it in a completely different perspective. He assumed full responsibility for that slaughter. "I have occasioned the death of all the persons of thy father's house" (v. 22). If David were interviewed following that news, he probably would have had a different view on the propriety of telling a lie for the sake of a single situation. The modern proponents of situational ethics fail to look beyond a given situation. Very rarely is a single situation of life an end unto itself. For this reason, the teaching that a deed is right or wrong in the light of that situation alone is most tragic and misleading. The Bible always exhorts the individual to truth, and this should be the practice of all believers in all ages, turning over all situations to God for the disposition of His will.

It is interesting to note that on an earlier occasion, Saul kept Agag, king of the Amalekites, and many sheep alive as an evi-

dence of his religious fervor, but now he lowered himself to the
mass slaughter of Israelite priests. One wonders whether or not
some of the men of Israel did not have second thoughts about
the monarchy at this point. Samuel had clearly warned the people that the day would come when the young men would be
appointed "runners" before the king, and now they were commanded to not only be runners before the king, but to participate in the mass slaughter of their own people.

The presence of Abiathar with David must have been of considerable comfort at this time, for now he had the ephod and the
Urim and the Thummim (23:6). In spite of the destruction and
devastation at Nob, God had made provision for David. This,
indeed, was an act of mercy and grace. Abiathar remained with
David for a long period of time, and after David's time as an
outlaw was appointed high priest. He held the office until Solomon banished him for his share in Adonijah's attempt at seizing
the throne (I Kings 2:26ff.).

II. A HERO WITHOUT A HOME (23:1—26:26)

A. *The Rescue of Keilah* (23:1-13)

While in the Hebron area, word came to David that the Philistines were planning a campaign in the Shephelah against the
city of Keilah which was located northwest of Hebron, about
thirteen miles east of the Philistines' stronghold of Gath. This
raid was to take place in the early summer, since they planned to
"rob the threshingfloors" (v. 1). The spiritual maturity and sensitivity of David was evident in the fact that he immediately inquired of the Lord before undertaking this war in spite of the
fact that such defense would have been perfectly legitimate. The
Lord's answer was positive, and David was commanded to go
and to protect the inhabitants of Keilah. The 600 men who
were with David, however, were very apprehensive about this
plan, for they feared reprisal from the men in Judah. It is evident from the third verse that the greater majority of the people
were still faithful to the crown and would help Saul against David. Again David inquired of the Lord (v. 4) and the answer
remained the same with the assurance that victory would come
because of the Lord's help. They encountered the Philistines

THE ADVENTURES OF A FUGITIVE   83

and won a decisive victory, even capturing cattle which belonged to the Philistines (v. 5). Following the battle, Abiathar,
the priest, joined David and brought with him the sacred ephod
(vv. 6-9). Even though David had saved the city, he was not
able to remain there because of the loyalty of many of its inhabitants to Saul (vv. 11-12). David then departed with his men
and abode in the wilderness of Ziph (v. 14).

B. *From the Wilderness to En-gedi* (23:14—24:22)

The rugged mountains in the wilderness of Ziph just south of
Hebron provided a good hiding place for David, whose life was
in danger every day as a result of Saul's pursuit (v. 14). In this
time of emotional and physical crisis, the Lord once again provided for David's needs. Jonathan, Saul's son, went to David in
that rugged territory and assured him that he would not be slain
at the hand of Saul (v. 17). Even more important was the recognition on Jonathan's part that David would be king over Israel
and Jonathan would be below him. To seal this agreement, a
covenant was made (v. 18).

The inhabitants of the wilderness of Ziph were loyal to Saul,
and went to him informing the king of David's travels in that
countryside. The king requested that they come back with a
more specific location, which they did. And Saul went down to
the wilderness of Ziph only to find that David had gone further
southward to the wilderness of Maon (v. 24). Saul and his men,
probably numbering approximately 3,000, were able to surround
David, and it appeared that the situation was very dark for this
man who had been promised the kingdom; however, providentially, the Lord stepped in, for a messenger came to Saul with
the news that the Philistines had invaded the land (v. 27). Evidently the Philistines had heard of Saul's interest in David in
the wilderness, and took this opportunity to invade the central
portion of Palestine. Saul had no alternative but to return to
the north and confront the Philistines, which decision, of course,
permitted David to escape once again. And once again we are
impressed with the unique and unending providential care of
God for His anointed.

From here David fled eastward to the wilderness of En-gedi

(see map, p. 76). After Saul's encounter with the Philistines, he received word of David's move to En-gedi, and immediately dispatched troops numbering 3,000 to go to that site. Saul, while wandering through the wilderness of that area, went into a cave to "cover his feet."[55] What Saul did not know was that David and some of his men were in the cave. Some of David's servants encouraged him to put an end to Saul's life, which David refused to do; but he did cut off part of the outer skirt of Saul (v. 4). This act brought no great joy to David, for his heart "smote him" in that he had mistreated God's anointed (cf. v. 5). David recognized that this deed was of his own bidding and not that which was commanded by God. In addition to that fact, David was very sensitive to the sanctity of the throne. As far as David was concerned, Saul was still God's anointed. Nowhere had the Lord indicated that it was his time to assume the throne. In the light of these facts, David considered his act most inappropriate. When Saul was awakened, David reminded him of the opportunity that he had to take his life (v. 10), and David pleaded with Saul to discontinue the constant search for his life. David even attempted to put the whole act of the king in full perspective when he asked him, ". . . after whom dost thou pursue? after a dead dog, after a flea?" (v. 14). A dog, especially of the wild variety, was that which roamed through the streets as scavengers and was considered the lowest of creatures in a Palestinian town. One can only imagine what the value of a dead dog might be in the light of that expression (cf. II Sam. 9:8). He also likened himself to a flea. This, of course, was done to show the ridiculousness of Saul's pursuit. For a king of Israel to pursue one with no more standing than a flea would indeed, involve a complete waste of time (cf. I Sam. 26:20).

When David completed his argument, Saul was overcome with emotion and lifted up his voice and wept. Even with his arrogant, belligerent attitude, Saul recognized the mercy of David (vv. 17-19). In the light of this he asked for a covenant that David would swear not to slay his household when he became

---

[55]A euphemism for "to relieve himself" or "to have bowel movement" (cf. Judg. 3:24).

king (vv. 20-21). To this David agreed, and the two evidently parted with those words.

C. *David and Nabal* (25:1-44)

1. *The Death of Samuel* (v. 1)

Samuel's death must have occurred sometime after the events at En-gedi, and for that reason is included in the narrative at this point. The fact that "all the Israelites" were gathered together and lamented for him indicates that he was very popular and well accepted in all Israel. He was buried in his house at Ramah, perhaps in the courtyard of his house, or possibly in a special burial chamber constructed for him.

2. *David at Carmel* (vv. 2-44)

The town of Carmel is located about three miles south of Hebron in the territory of Maon. Living in that city was a man by the name of Nabal whose name in Hebrew means "fool." He is described in verse 3 as a "churlish" man (Heb. *qāšeh* — "hard, severe") and evil in his ways. Nabal was evidently a man of considerable means, for David sent ten of his young men to his house to ask for help. When the men arrived there, they were given something less than a royal welcome. The sarcasm and the insults of Nabal were quickly relayed to David (cf. vv. 8-12). When David heard these things, his immediate response was to arm his men and go up and take that which they wanted by force (v. 13). While David exhibited some impatience at this point, he learned an important lesson and later exhibited great patience (cf. II Sam. 16:11-12). The servants of Nabal were very frustrated by their master's lack of insight. They immediately went to Abigail, Nabal's wife, and reported the events of that day to her. The lack of respect on the part of the servants is evident in their description of their master, for they classify him as a "son of Belial" (v. 17). Abigail immediately made preparations to intervene and to mediate what appeared to be a disastrous situation. Her arguments and her wisdom were most impressive to David, so much so that after the death of Nabal, David took her to become his wife (vv. 39-42). He probably did this due to the fact that Michal, Saul's daughter, had been given to another man (cf. v. 44); however, that David's practices involved polygamy is made quite clear by the information found in verse 43.

D. *Saul's Life Again Spared* (26:1-25)

Because of the similarities between this chapter and Chapter 24, many critics regard the two stories as duplicate versions of the same incident. It should be pointed out, however, that the differences outweigh the resemblances, and the difficulty of reconciling the narratives, if they refer to the same occurrence, is far greater than that of supposing that somewhat similar events happened twice.

For the second time the Ziphites were the informers as to David's location (v. 1; cf. 23:19). Saul took 3,000 men with him and sought David in the wilderness of Ziph (v. 2). David heard of Saul's move and sent out his own spies in an attempt to locate Saul and to observe his movements. Among the soldiers of David was a certain Ahimelech, a Hittite. The presence of a Hittite among David's men indicates that he had a number of foreign mercenaries serving in his band of 600. David was able to locate Saul in the camp of Israel by virtue of the fact that Saul had a spear "stuck in the ground at his bolster." A better translation of this phrase would be "his spear stuck in the ground at his head." The spear was the symbol of authority in place of the scepter. This is the reason that the spear ("javelin" — A.V.) was at hand in the royal court of Saul (cf. I Sam. 18:8ff.; 19:9). This traditional sign of authority still exists among some bedouin Arabs today. A spear stuck in the ground outside the entrance, distinguishes the tent of the sheikh. Abishai considered this the opportune time to take the life of Saul (v. 8). But again, David was very sensitive to the fact that Saul was still God's anointed, and to attempt assassination would be out of the will of God (v. 9). Perhaps David had the law of Exodus 22:28 in mind, "You shall not defile God, nor curse a ruler of your people" (RSV). David's patience, spiritual insight, and deep sense of faithfulness to the crown is unparalleled in ancient history. David, perhaps, fully recognized that if assassination were carried out here, what guarantee would he have that it would not become a practice when he took the throne?

In order to demonstrate how close Saul came to death, a spear and a water container were taken from Saul's side (v. 11). This was all made possible because a deep sleep from the Lord had fallen upon Saul and his servants (v. 12). After they were a good distance away, David called out to Abner, who was the king's personal guard that night (v. 14; cf. v. 5). David's chiding of Abner's inability to guard the king awakened Saul (cf. vv. 15-16). A dialogue then began between Saul and David, and once again David reminded Saul of the opportunities he had to take his life. David also pointed out to Saul the great inconvenience which he had suffered as a result of Saul's attitude. His own countrymen had made him a man without a country, and in driving him from Israel, they left him only with the alternative "to serve other gods" (v. 19). Perhaps the people suggested this because once having left Israel and the sanctuary, they felt the only way to worship would be to worship the gods of that foreign land. Once again David likened himself to a flea, and tried to impress Saul with the futility of his searches (v. 20). David also likened Saul's pursuit as a partridge hunt in the mountains. It is appropriate that the illustration used here made reference to the partridge hunt in Palestine. The nature of the hunt paralleled quite accurately the situation of David. The common species of partridge in the Holy Land attempts to save himself by running rather than by flight. The bird is continually chased until it is fatigued; then it is knocked down with sticks thrown along the ground. This, in a very vivid way, reflects the nature of Saul's pursuit. Even more interesting is the fact that he likened Saul's actions to a partridge hunt *in the mountains* which would not generally be the case. Who would hunt a single partridge which had flown into the mountains or had run there when they may be found in large coveys in the fields below?

David's respect for the throne of Israel is further in evidence in the fact that he returned the king's spear. This spear, of course, was a sign of authority, and even though David had been anointed to the throne, again it was not the right time. David was fully committed to the will of God, and refused to usurp the throne that had been promised to him.

III. RETURN TO PHILISTIA (27:1-12)

The faith of David at this stage in his career reached a very low point. He had given up any hope of reconciliation with the royal court (v. 1). The only option that he saw open was to return to the land of the enemy, for there perhaps he could find a place of rest. Thus, David with his band of 600 fighting men returned to the city of Gath which seems to be a rather unusual decision on his part since he had been previously turned away from that site (v. 2; cf. 21:10-15), but some time had elapsed and David's status as an outlaw or a fugitive had been well established in Philistia as well as in the hills of Judah, thus making it possible to come to Achish, the king of Gath, and request allegiance and protection. Achish, of course, was more than happy to accommodate David, for he knew of David's skill as a warrior and was convinced that David could be a great help in his attempts to conquer Israelite territory.

David was suspicious of permanently residing near or in the royal court of Achish and requested a territory of his own in the countryside (v. 5). This he did so he would be free from the constant surveillance to which he would be exposed in the capital city. Also, David probably wanted freedom to observe his own religious rites. David's decision also may have involved his attempt to protect his followers from assimilation with Philistine religious ideas and customs. The fact that David was accepted by the Philistines probably indicates that he was similar to the typical *Habiru* of Canaan. Also, it is entirely probable that Achish was in desperate need of reinforcements following his encounter with King Saul (cf. 23:27-28).

The year and four months (v. 7) that David dwelt among the Philistines provided him with many opportunities to help his countrymen in Judah. David took this opportunity to destroy some of the enemies of Judah; and such victories, by their very nature, had to be complete in order that survivors could not inform the king of Gath regarding the nature of David's raids (cf. vv. 9-12).

David's experiences among the Philistines would have further consequences, however. When he would become king, he would have considerable knowledge of Philistine geography and military tactics, which would be a decided advantage in planning attacks and conquering their territory. Again we have an excellent example of God's providential preparation of a man. In many respects, David's time in Philistia was parallel to Moses' days in Egypt. While Saul's pursuit of David was fully intended for evil, God meant it for good (cf. Gen. 50:20).

Chapter 7

A VOICE FROM THE DEAD

(I Samuel 28)

Saul's preoccupation with the pursuit of David through the hills of Judah could not but help to have military implications for Israel. In all probability Saul gave little attention to the growing Philistine threat since his concentration was centered on David and his men. Word certainly reached Achish, king of Gath, and other kings of Philistia relative to the mental and spiritual problems in Saul's life. Achish was convinced that with David and his men numbered among his forces he had a decided advantage in planning an attack against Israel. He was sure that David was now the enemy of Israel (27:12) and would seize upon an opportunity to gain revenge against Saul. From the standpoint of Israel's strength, prospects were dark indeed. Saul had become a man of unpredictable temperament and preoccupied with the preservation of his personal dignity. This caused him to neglect crucial problems within the borders of Israel. In addition to that, one of his more capable warriors, David, was now fighting with the enemy. Perhaps even more frustrating to Saul was his inability to get divine help.

Chapter 28 of the book of I Samuel records one of the darkest hours of Saul's reign. This chapter is a startling contrast with the earlier chapters of I Samuel where a young, energetic, heroic king is described. The vitality and strength of Saul had been stripped away by divine judgment (16:14). As the Philistine army units began to mobilize in preparation for an encounter with Israel, Saul trembled perhaps as he had never trembled before. It was this situation that led Saul to seek help from a "witch" (necromancer) located in the north at En-dor.

I. THE PLIGHT OF SAUL (28:1-6)

A. *The Philistine Menace* (28:1-5)

As the Philistines mobilized their troops for warfare, Achish gave David the order that he was to join him in battle (v. 1).

This situation was indeed most awkward for David, for it meant he would have to fight his own people. In the light of David's past performances with regard to Saul, it is quite clear that he would not actually fight against Israel. For if he refused to take the life of Saul, it follows that he would not participate in a battle which would bring the death of his fellow countrymen. However, it was not possible for David to refuse outright the command of this king, for in so doing he would not only jeopardize his own life, but the lives of his men; therefore, with intentional ambiguity he responded by saying, "Surely thou shalt know what thy servant can do" (v. 2). Achish was satisfied with the answer and promised to give David a special position in his court. In this situation David had no alternative but to rely on divine intervention for a way of escape. Somewhat parenthetically, the writer inserted two important facts necessary to our understanding of the rest of the chapter. First, he noted that Samuel was dead and, as a matter of fact, had been dead for some time (25:1). Second, Saul had put out of the country those who had "familiar spirits."

The Philistines continued to organize their armies and moved northward to the site of Shunem (v. 4). This site is now known as Solem, about three miles north of Jezreel at the southern base of the hill of Moreh across the valley from Mt. Gilboa. The very fact that the Philistines could move freely to such a location and occupy the site indicates something of Saul's neglect with regard to the defense of Israel's borders. Certainly the presence of the Philistines in that area was a serious threat to the tribes of Issachar, Zebulun and Asher. David evidently remained with the Philistines during this period of time and probably hoped for an opportunity to remove himself from the battle or, if that failed, to turn on the Philistines and become an ally of the Israelites. In all probability Saul, by means of his scouts, had received word that David was with the Philistine forces encamped in the north. This, plus the absence of Samuel, probably accounted for Saul's desperate move recorded in the remaining part of this chapter.

B. *The Silence of God* (28:6)

With a major confrontation with the Philistines drawing near, Saul "enquired of the Lord." The heavens, however, were silent

at this time. Some might regard this as a harsh or unjust act on
the part of God, but it should be remembered that in the past
Saul had many opportunities to discover the will of God. He had
openly refused prophetic commands (I Sam. 10:8) and had
murdered the priests of the sanctuary at Nob (22:9-23). Since
Saul had voluntarily chosen to follow his own counsel, God permitted him to reap the fruit of such sowing (cf. Gal. 6:7).

Some have suggested that there is a contradiction between
this verse and I Chronicles 10:14. The latter text suggests that
Saul "enquired not of the Lord," whereas the Samuel passage
states that he did inquire of the Lord. In the Samuel passage
we are given no hint as to the means that Saul used for such inquiry or the attitude that existed at the time of inquiry. The
passage in I Chronicles appears to be a divine interpretation of
the situation. In a real sense Saul did not inquire of the Lord
with a repentant heart, and therefore the inquiry was not a
legitimate one.

The three means by which the will of God was discerned during this period were: (1) dreams, (2) Urim and (3) prophetic
revelation. Dreams were often used by God as a means of special
communication (cf. Gen. 20:6; 37:5-10; 41:7-32; I Kings 3:5; Dan.
2:3-45; 4:5-19; Matt. 1:20). Dreams were apparently common
to the Mosaic era and those interpreting dreams had to be carefully screened (cf. Deut. 13:1, 3, 5).

The second means of divine communication involved the Urim
(Heb. *'urîm* — "lights"). A complete identification and function
of the Urim and Thummim (Heb. *tummîm* — "perfection") is
difficult because of the limited number of references to them and
their use. They were associated with the breastplate of the high
priest (cf. Exod. 28:30; Lev. 8:8). During times of national crisis the high priest was called and judgment was sought by means
of the Urim (Num. 27:21). The Urim and Thummim were commonly used in the Mosaic period and the early days of the
United Monarchy. The use of these objects seems to have de-
clined or ceased until the post-exilic period when they are again
mentioned.[56] There is a wide variety of views as to the particu-

---

[56]Hosea 3:4 may be a possible exception.

lar form or identity of the Urim and Thummim. Josephus identified them with the twelve stones in the breastplate of the high
priest. He suggested that the stones were illuminated thus giving
divine information prior to the time of battle.[57] A Talmudic explanation suggests that certain letters appeared on the stone in
the breastplate and were illuminated at the moment of revelation, thus giving the high priest an indication of God's will.
Other scholars feel that there was nothing in the object themselves that revealed the divine will, but they were merely sym-
bols of God's revelation. When a problem was presented to the
high priest, he merely laid the matter before God in prayer and
by means of inspiration received the answer. More recent discussion on the subject attempts to identify the Urim and Thummim
as two flat objects (stones). On one side of each was the word
Urim, derived from the Hebrew root 'ārar — "to curse"; the other side was marked Thummim ("perfect" = "yes"). When both
Urim sides appeared, the answer was negative, and when both
the Thummim sides appeared, the answer was positive. The
identification of the Urim and Thummim with the sacred lots
appears to have some possibilities, but there are serious difficulties with this view due to the fact that the answers ascribed to the
Urim and Thummim are not always the equivalent to a yes or no
answer (cf. Judg. 1:2; 20:18; I Sam. 22:10; II Sam. 5:23; 21:1).[58]
Regardless of the precise nature of the Urim and Thummim it is
clear that Saul did not have access to the original objects at this
time, for since the slaughter of the priests at Nob, the high priest,
Abiathar, with the ephod had been in David's camp (cf. 22:20ff.;
23:6; 30:7). It is, of course, not impossible that Saul appointed a
new priest and made a new ephod with Urim and Thummim.
If this were the case, it would further explain why God refused to
respond to Saul's inquiry.

[57]*Ant.* III.8.9.

[58]For further discussion of the problem see J. A. Motyer, "Urim and
Thummim," *The New Bible Dictionary,* J. D. Douglas, ed. (Grand Rapids:
William B. Eerdmans Publishing Company, 1962), p. 1306 and Nathan
Isaacs, "Urim and Thummim," *The International Standard Bible En-
cyclopedia,* James Orr, ed., (Grand Rapids: William B. Eerdmans Publishing
Company, 1960), V, p. 3040.

Village of Endor. Matson Photo Service

II. SAUL AND THE WITCH OF EN-DOR (28:7-25)

A. *Witchcraft in the Ancient Near East.*

The concept that information from a deity could be gained by means of outward signs was not uncommon in ancient Greece, Egypt, Babylon, and Palestine. The Old Testament makes reference to at least six forms of divination. All these, however, were clearly condemned as inappropriate to the search for God's will. They are as follows: (1) Hepatoscopy, which was the process of divining from the liver of a sacrificed animal (cf. Ezek. 21:21). That this was a common practice not only in Babylon, but also in Palestine is evident from the discovery of clay models of livers found at Megiddo and elsewhere. (2) Hydromancy, or divination by water. Many feel that this is referred to in the Joseph story (Gen. 44:5). (3) Rhabdomancy. This refers to the use of a divining rod or the casting of arrows (cf. Ezek. 21:21; Hos. 4: 12). (4) Teraphim. The use of teraphim or household images was quite common among the peoples of Mesopotamia and Palestine. They were a sign of authority and land ownership, but were also used for purposes of divination (cf. Ezek. 21:21; Zech. 10:2). (5) Astrology. The study of the stars rests upon the belief that the heavenly bodies are in fact deities or are controlled by deities and influence the destiny of men. Those who study the stars and their various patterns claim to understand the future of individuals. Such a practice was very common to Babylon and appeared to be a problem in the days of the prophets (Isa. 47:13; Jer. 10:2). (6) Necromancy. Necromancy includes two ideas. One involves the worship of ancestors and the other is that the dead may be consulted for purposes of determining the future. The practice of necromancy is uniformally forbidden in the Old Testament (see Lev. 19:31; Deut. 18:11; Isa. 8:19; 19:3). While Saul had apparently driven out many who practiced consultation with the dead (cf. I Sam. 28:3), some individuals continued to live and practice their craft within the borders of Israel.

B. *The Woman with a Familiar Spirit* (28:7-11)

In his desperation to seek an omen for the future, Saul commanded that a woman be sought out who could consult the dead.

The Hebrew text describes such a woman as follows: *'ešat ba-'alat 'ôḇ*. "The Hebrew word *'ôḇ* may refer to a 'skin-bottle' or a necromancer."[59] Its usage in this context is quite clearly a reference to departed spirits or subterranean spirits. A woman practicing such witchcraft was discovered at the site of En-dor, south of Mt. Tabor, about eight miles from where Saul was staying with his forces on Mt. Gilboa. Saul disguised himself as a common Israelite and contacted the woman at night, the only time that necromancy could be practiced because of Saul's previous action (v. 8; cf. v. 3). When the woman expressed apprehension in fullfilling Saul's request, he swore that the whole thing would be kept secret and her safety would be assured (v. 10). The request of Saul was that Samuel the prophet be brought back from the dead in order that communication might be established (v. 11).

C. *The Appearance of Samuel* (28:12-19)

The appearance of Samuel on this occasion has created a great deal of discussion among Bible scholars and has produced a number of viewpoints with regard to the precise nature of this event. They are as follows: (1) The appearance of Samuel was not a literal one, but merely the product of psychological impressions. According to this view the woman had permitted herself to become emotionally involved and psychologically identified with the prophet so that she was convinced that he had actually appeared when called. Daniel Erdmann describes this approach as follows:

> This can be explained psychologically only as by an inner vision, the occasion for which was given by Saul's request to bring up Samuel, and the psychological foundation of which was her inward excitement, in connection with her lively recollection of Samuel's form, which was well known to her from his earthly life, and stood before her mind in vividest distinctness.[60]

---

[59]Francis Brown, S. R. Driver, and Charles Briggs, *A Hebrew and English Lexicon of the Old Testament* (Oxford: The Clarendon Press, Corrected Impression, 1952), p. 15.

[60]"The Books of Samuel," *Lange's Commentary*, Philip Schaff, ed., (Grand Rapids: Zondervan Publishing House, 1960), V, p. 336.

Two objections can be raised against this view. The first is derived from verse 12 which indicates that when Samuel did appear the medium cried out with a loud voice, apparently surprised or startled by his appearance. Such would not be the case if she were merely seeking a vision produced by "psychological excitement." Second, the general reading of the text leads one to the conclusion that not only did the woman speak with Samuel, but Saul spoke with him as well (cf. v. 15).

(2) A demon or Satan impersonated Samuel. Those holding this view argue for the idea that a visible form of Samuel himself appeared, but which was in reality merely an impersonation of him.[61] Many who defend this view argue that God would not permit a woman of this type to actually disturb the rest of a godly man. The whole affair is therefore considered a satanic or demonic deception of Saul. The advocates of this view remind us that Satan can appear as "an angel of light" (II Cor. 11:14) and, therefore, has the ability to carry out such deceptions. In evaluating this view, it should be pointed out that the basic reading of the Biblical text leads one to the conclusion that this was actually Samuel and not an impersonation. While it is true that Satan can perform such deception, it is highly doubtful that he has the prophetic knowledge necessary to reveal that which was given to Saul in this chapter. Furthermore, if this were a demon or an evil spirit, it is improbable that he would have given the prediction found in this passage. More likely, in the light of the godly character of David and the wickedness of Saul, the demonic power would have flattered Saul with a positive prophecy.

(3) The whole thing was a deliberate imposture practiced upon Saul. The witch really did not see Samuel, but fooled Saul into believing that her voice or that of someone else was that of Samuel. Those maintaining this view point out that only the woman saw Samuel and reported his words. Saul heard and saw nothing. The following is a representative argument for this view:

---

[61]Merrill F. Unger, *Biblical Demonology* (Wheaton: Van Kampen Press, Inc., 1952), p. 150. Cf. also Matthew Henry, *Commentary on the Holy Bible*, II, p. 767.

The more reasonable view is that the whole transaction was a feigning on the part of the woman. The LXX uses the word *eggastrimuthos* (a ventriloquist) to describe the woman and those who exercise kindred arts (v. 9). Though pretending ignorance (v. 12) the woman doubtless recognizes Saul from the first. It was she who saw Samuel, and reported his words; the king himself saw and heard nothing. It required no great skill in a practical diviner to forecast the general issue of the battle about to take place, and the disaster which would overtake Saul and his sons; while if the forecast had proved untrue, the narrative would never have been written. Saul, in fact, was not slain, but killed himself. The incident, therefore, may best be ranked in the same category as the feats of modern mediumship.[62]

A number of objections may be raised against this view. In the first place, the Bible does not specifically say that the woman reported Samuel's words; on the contrary, it makes it clear that Samuel spoke directly to Saul. Orr's statement that the king "saw and heard nothing" is in direct conflict with the obvious reading of the text (cf. v. 15ff.). It is also highly doubtful that she was in a position to predict the outcome of the battle and specifically forecast the death of Saul's sons. It is also unlikely, from a practical point of view, that she would give such a forecast to a man obviously aligned with the Israelite camp.

(4) The most popular view and that which is maintained by most orthodox commentators is that this was a genuine appearance of Samuel brought about by God himself. In favor of this proposal is the Septuagint reading of I Chronicles 10:13 which is as follows: "Saul asked counsel of her that had a familiar spirit to inquire of her, and Samuel made answer to him." Furthermore, the fact that she cried out when she saw Samuel indicated that she did not bring up Samuel and did not expect him to appear in this manner. The fact that Saul bowed himself to the ground and did obeisance is a further indication that this was a real appearance of Samuel. It is doubtful that he would have reacted merely on the grounds of a verbal description or a false

---

[62]James Orr, "Witch of Endor," *The International Standard Bible Encyclopedia,* II, p. 944.

impression. Samuel's statement to Saul in verse 15 should not be regarded as a proof of the fact that the witch of En-dor or Saul brought him back from the dead.[63]

What, then, was the purpose of God in bringing Samuel back for this appearance? This unusual act on the part of God was certainly designed to emphasize the doom of Saul and God's displeasure for his coming to a necromancer. Robert Jamieson suggests three additional reasons: (1) To make Saul's crime an instrument of his punishment, (2) to show the heathen world God's superiority in prophecy, and (3) to confirm a belief in a future state after death.[64]

Two other men who made an appearance on the earth after death were Moses and Elijah at the transfiguration of Christ (Matt. 17:3; Luke 9:30, 31). They, however, appeared "in glory," but Samuel appeared in the mantle which he had worn while on earth. Therefore, in a real sense the appearance of Samuel after death was a completely unique event.

Since occultism and necromancy are again enjoying popular acceptance, it might be well to sound a note of warning at this point. There are many well-meaning persons who are being led into a very subtle trap regarding these practices. It is clear from Scripture that the believer is not to participate in any practice of this kind (Lev. 19:31; Deut. 18:10-14). Basically, physical death envolves the separation of the soul from the body. That soul is then committed into the hands of a sovereign God and remains either in the presence of Christ or in the confines of Hades. The Bible makes it clear that the next major event involving that individual is the judgment (Heb. 9:27). The Bible nowhere hints that individuals on earth can contact or communicate with those who have departed. It is also clear that believers in the intermediate state are in a condition of "rest" or "comfort" which could hardly be said if they were capable of being called to return to the earth by mediums (cf. Luke 16:25; Rev. 6:11).

[63]On this point see Christian Wordsworth, *The Holy Bible with Notes* (London: Revington's, 1873), II, Part II, p. 63.

[64]"I Samuel," *Commentary on the Whole Bible,* Jamieson, Fausset and Brown, eds. (Grand Rapids: William B. Eerdmans Publishing Co., 1948), II, p. 211.

It is even more doubtful that God would permit such individuals, whether in His presence or in Hades, to be called back to earth for superficial reasons which are usually given for such communication.

The account of Lazarus and the rich man provides some important information on this subject. It is asserted that between the believer and unbeliever is a great "gulf" fixed which cannot be crossed (Luke 16:26). It is also evident from the story that those who have departed are not able to return to earth for any reason (cf. Luke 16:28-31). It would be a tragic thing indeed if the souls of believers could be brought back from the presence of Christ by an unbelieving medium here on earth for the mere purpose of attending to the sentimentality of a relative.

D. *Saul's Sorrow* (28:20-25)

The stern condemnation of Samuel was all too clear to Saul, and the future was now apparent to him. He wanted to know the disposition of events in the immediate future — now he knew them. He also knew well the divine reason for disapproval (28: 18). The scene before us is a tragic and pitiful one indeed, for on the ground lies a man, once known for his heroic deeds as a soldier, one who had been filled with the Spirit of God, one who had a bright future ahead of him. All of this now was lost because of rebellion against and contempt for God's will. The woman tried to console Saul as best she could. A meal was provided for Saul and his servants, but he refused to eat until he was compelled (v. 23). Food and physical comfort now seemed insignificant to Saul, for on the horizon he could see the ominous, black clouds of death beginning to gather. His hours and days were numbered; the end was not far away.

Chapter 8

THE END OF AN ERA
(I Samuel 29—31)

The final chapters of the book of I Samuel describe one of the saddest stories of ancient Hebrew history. Approximately forty years earlier a young man from the tribe of Benjamin was chosen and anointed by Samuel as Israel's first king. He was a man with physical strength and military capability. The legal, spiritual and military fortunes of Israel were placed upon his shoulders; but one thing was not taken into account on the part of Israel in those early days of optimism. Samuel sounded a warning concerning the danger of putting trust in human capacity alone. The real success of Israel did not lie in her production of capable men, but in her faith in Jehovah, as well as complete obedience to His revelation. The tragic events recorded in the concluding chapters of the book of I Samuel are in direct contrast to the optimism and enthusiasm of the tribes recorded in I Samuel 10. When Saul was selected king and publicly recognized as such at Mizpeh, the future indeed looked bright, at least from a human point of view. Saul appeared to be the man of the hour, a man with the promise of a bright future. As the book of I Samuel concludes, however, Saul is viewed in a heap, wounded and bleeding on Mt. Gilboa. Disobedience and constant insensitivity to the will of God led to this tragic end.

The final chapters of this interesting book are not exclusively devoted to a pessimistic outlook for Israel. One is able to see the providential deliverance of David from a rather awkward and delicate situation, thus vindicating the promise of God that David would be the next king.

I. DAVID AND ACHISH (29:1-11)

A. *The Mobilization of the Philistines* (29:1-5)

The historical narrative found in this chapter continues that which was begun in 28:2. The march of the Philistine armies led them northward to Aphek which has not been definitely located, for there are a number of towns with this name. The Israelite armies located their camp by a fountain which was in Jezreel. That fountain is usually identified with the present Ain-Jalud located at the foot of Gilboa. Battle preparations were carried out by the Philistines by organizing their forces into companies of hundreds and thousands (v. 2). The principal leaders of the organization were the "lords of the Philistines" (v. 2 — Heb. *sarnê pelistîm*; cf. Josh. 13:3 and I Sam. 6:16). David, along with Achish, formed the rear guard.

As military organization continued, the "princes of the Philistines" (Heb. *sārê pelistîm*) noticed that Hebrews were among the Philistine forces. The princes mentioned in this verse are to be distinguished from the principal leaders of the march mentioned in verse 2. Evidently the princes were company leaders who immediately recognized the presence of David and his men. Their use of the term "Hebrew" to identify an Israelite is in agreement with other uses in the Old Testament. The term "Hebrew" was used commonly by foreigners to identify an Israelite. Achish was very quick to defend the presence of David and his men by reminding the princes that David had been with him for a long time and had served him faithfully. The argument of Achish was less than convincing, however, and the military leaders demanded that David return. Their concern is expressed in the latter part of verse 4. The original text is of some interest here. The commanders were concerned that in the heat of battle David, rather than being an ally, would turn on them and become an "adversary." The Hebrew term for adversary is *sātān* ("satan"). The use of the term *sātān* in this context is enlightening, for it gives important insight into the character and deceitfulness of the adversary of the believer. An adversary, as described in this context, would be one who would make out to be an ally, but at a crucial time would turn and bring disaster. This is precisely the Apostle Paul's characterization of Satan, the adversary of the believer (cf. II Cor. 11:14; I Tim. 5:14). The princes remembered well the exploits of David and, in particular, his defeat of Goliath. They also remembered the popular folk tune which was well known not only to the Israelites, but evidently to the Philistines as well (v. 5; cf. 18:7; 21:11).

B. *The Return of David* (29:6-11)

Achish realized that the military leaders were serious in their demands. Since he could not afford to risk his political future for the sake of David and his men, he told David to return to his hometown. The words of Achish as recorded in Scripture are somewhat problematic, for in his attempt to emphasize the innocence of David, he employed the expression "as the Lord liveth." This appears to be a strange statement coming from the lips of a heathen king. Scholars have tended to interpret this expression in three different ways: (1) Some feel that Achish may have been attracted to Israel's religion through his association with David and, therefore, would have used the expression quite naturally. (2) Others feel that Achish actually used a different expression, but the writer used a substitution in preparing the final record of these events. (3) The more probable view proposed by S. Goldman is that Achish used this expression basically to impress David with his sincerity.[65] The very fact that Achish had found no deceit in David gives some indication of David's skill as both a warrior and politician while living in the land of the enemy. The raids which he conducted gave every appearance of being favorable to Philistine interest, but in essence were in defense of the land of Judah.

David was very diplomatic in his response to the words of Achish, for quickly to agree with Achish's command would be to raise questions concerning his loyalty to the Philistine cause. But to object to it too vigorously might lead to engagement in the Philistine battle with Israel which would place him in a most awkward position indeed! Thus, very diplomatically, David reacted with surprise and indignation that his loyalty should be questioned. Inwardly he certainly must have rejoiced at the deliverance from the dilemma in which he found himself (v. 8). The mild reaction of David satisfied Achish that David was truly an ally, but he continued to remind David that while he was a man without guilt he still could not participate in the Philistine battle. It appears that Achish was rather knowledgeable of Israelite customs and literary idioms, for in describing the inno-

---

[65]*Op. cit.*, p. 174.

cence of David he referred to him as "an angel of God." This seems to have been a common Hebrew expression of this period (cf. II Sam. 14:17; 19:27).

The words of Achish recorded in verse 10 have been somewhat perplexing to expositors, for it seems that David is described as a subject of Saul rather then a vassal-servant of the Philistines. The expression "thy master's servants" (Heb. 'aḇdê 'aḏōnèkā) is better translated "the servants of your lord," a clear reference to King Saul. Why would Achish refer to David and his men in this manner? Several suggestions have been offered in solution to the problem. H. D. M. Spence's explanation is as follows:

> It is hardly the expression we should expect Achish to use of David's followers. All Israelites were, of course, "subjects of Saul," but the term would hardly be used except of one hostile to David, as Nabal was: he once (25:10) made use of an insulting term of a like nature to David. Achish we know, seemed ever kindly disposed to the outlaw son of Jesse. A probable suggestion has, however, been lately made, that the reference here is to those tribes of Manasseh (cf. I Chron. 12:19-21) who had only lately come over to David. Was it not also possible that these very Manassites, who had only very recently deserted the king's cause for David's, were known to some of the Philistines as Saul's soldiers, and that their suspicion had been awakened in the first place by finding them marching under David's standard in the division of Gath?[66]

Another writer suggests that ". . . the use of these terms may suggest that Achish did not consider David his vassal any longer, but delicately intimated that David was at liberty to leave Philistia if he so desired."[67] It is entirely possible, of course, that Achish used the expression in a purely non-political sense, referring, perhaps, to David's ethnic relationship, rather than his political commitments.

II. THE DESTRUCTION OF ZIKLAG (30:1-31)

A. *The Amalekite Invasion* (30:1-5)

Three days after David left Achish he and his men approached

[66]*Op. cit.*, p. 421.
[67]Francis D. Nichol, *op. cit.*, p. 591.

the small town of Ziklag where they had resided. Rather than being received warmly by his friends and family, he discovered mass destruction and sorrow. The Amalekites, who wandered in the Negev district in great numbers, had taken advantage of David's absence to avenge themselves of his previous invasions and plundering (cf. 27:8). It will be remembered that Saul defeated these people in a major battle earlier, but failed to destroy them completely as commanded by God (I Sam. 15:2ff.). The Amalekites, in addition to destroying the city, had taken the women captives, probably to sell them in the Egyptian slave market. Those captured included David's two wives, Ahinoam the Jezreelitess and Abigail (v. 5). Adding to David's sorrow over this tragedy was the wrath of the people who evidently considered David's absence the cause of the disaster. Such public indignation was not new in Israel's history, for Moses experienced a similar reaction (cf. Exod. 17:4).

It seemed that in the darkest hours of tragedy and confusion David's spiritual countenance shone the brightest. Verse 6 indicates that in this hour of sorrow David "encouraged himself in the Lord his God." The Hebrew text is far more vivid at this point than is reflected in the Authorized Version. The translation should read, "but David strengthened himself in the Lord his God." David had complete confidence in the sovereignty of his God and immediately turned to the Lord for consolation and wisdom. The evidence of his faith is also observed in the procedure described in verse 7. David immediately called for Abiathar, the priest who had been with him since the messacre at Nob (cf. I Sam. 22:9-23; 23:9). As the high priest, of course, Abiathar had the sacred ephod which meant that inquiry by means of Urim and Thummim would be possible. It is interesting that David inquired of the Lord at all regarding this problem. It certainly gives rich insight into his spiritual sensitivity to the will of God. The most natural inclination would have been to take revenge on those who had destroyed the city, but David recognized that warfare included more than mere retaliatory acts. He did not want to jeopardize the lives of those who remained. The Lord assured David that he would be given a complete victory and instructed him to pursue the Amalekites (cf. vv. 8-10).

On the way south David encountered an Egyptian who described himself as a servant of an Amalekite (cf. vv. 11-13). The fact that an Egyptian was a slave to an Amalekite is very enlightening. It appears that the arrogant Amalekites had raided parts of Egypt and had taken slaves from there as well. The young Egyptian servant was ill and of no value to the master; so he had been left to die in the desert. David agreed to spare the life of this young man if he would reveal the location of the Amalekite forces. When David and his men reached the Amalekite camp, they found them spread across the desert eating, drinking and dancing in celebration of their victory over the towns in Judah (cf. v. 16). This extravagant victory celebration is reminiscent of one which was carried out in a later period of history by Benhadad I in the days of Ahab (cf. I Kings 20:15-20). David took advantage of this situation and his men rushed upon the Amalekites who were in no position to defend themselves. The victory was complete, allowing David to recover all that the Amalekites had taken from Ziklag (v. 18). The only ones to escape the destruction of David were four hundred young men who fled on camels (v. 17). Camels were evidently the principal method of mobilization used by the desert fighters throughout this period of time. One is reminded of the mobilized forces of the Midianites who also employed the camel for military use (cf. Judg. 6:5).

On the return back to Ziklag David was confronted with another very delicate problem. The men who actually participated in the battle numbered only four hundred. Two hundred of his men had to remain behind, perhaps because of exhaustion in the forced march southward (v. 9). Certain men among the four hundred felt that only those who actually fought in the battle should be the recipients of the spoil which they had recovered (v. 22). This viewpoint, however, reflected the very thing which David wanted to avoid, namely, assuming that victory came by human effort alone. David reminded his men that their victory had been given to them by the Lord (v. 23). David evidently used a precedent established by Moses to solve the problem. He reminded the men that the spoils belong to all the people of Israel, not only to those who fought in the battle (v. 24; cf. Num. 31:25-54). The decision of David evidently continued in force and became a military policy for many years in Israel (cf. II Macc. 8:28-30).

When David returned to Ziklag, he took a large portion of the spoils which he had recovered and sent it to the elders of Judah and to friends in various cities. This was an important move on David's part because it re-established contacts with the leaders of Judah. His act was perhaps a way of expressing gratitude for the protection they had afforded him in the hills of Judah when pursued by King Saul. Such an act would also be a means of demonstrating his loyalty to the people of Judah. This was made necessary because of his long association with the Philistines (a year and seven months). Among the towns to receive goods from David was the town of Hebron which was to become the capital of his first kingdom (v. 31).

III. THE DEATH OF SAUL AND JONATHAN (31:1-13)

A. *The Battle at Gilboa* (31:1-10)

Chapter 31 continues the history begun in 28:1. It was probably not very long after Saul's visit to En-dor that the battle took place. The Israelites had assumed that if they made Mt. Gilboa their final line of defense, they would be safe. They calculated that the Philistines would limit their battle to the valley of Jezreel and would not follow them into the mountains. This assumption, however, was a false one, for the Israelites were badly defeated in the field and the Philistines did pursue them into mountains of Gilboa. There the sons of Saul were slain. It is with a sense of sorrow that one reads of the death of Jonathan (v. 2). Among those associated with King Saul, he appeared to be the only one with practical insight and a deep love for David. Saul's son, Ish-bosheth, was evidently not involved in the battle (or escaped), for he survived to become king over Israel for a brief period of time (cf. II Sam. 2:8-10).

As the battle continued in the area surrounding Gilboa, Saul was struck by the archers (v. 3). The phrase "He was sore wounded of the archers" is better translated from the Hebrew text as "He was greatly alarmed regarding the archers." In all likelihood the Philistines had sent out a specially trained detachment to find Saul. The welfare of the king in battle was very important for the morale of the troops on both sides. A similar procedure was practiced by the Syrians in their conflict with Ahab and Jehoshaphat (II Chron. 18:28-34). Saul's great fear was that while still alive the Philistines would take him captive and abuse him to the shame of Israel (v. 4; cf. the treatment of Samson, Judg. 16:23-31). In desperation Saul asked his armorbearer to slay him so he would not be taken alive by the Philistines; but the armorbearer refused to do this, for he was afraid he would be seen killing the king and his own life would be taken. In complete frustration and fear Saul attempted to commit suicide by falling on his own sword. According to this narrative, Saul's death was occasioned by this event (v. 6). However, some question has been raised about the details of the narrative in the light of the Amalekite's story recorded in II Samuel. Many feel that Saul's ultimate death was brought about by the Amalekite. The various views on this problem will be dealt with in the next chapter.

When the Philistines finally got to Saul, they cut off his head, stripped off his armor and sent it into their principal cities. The cutting off of the head was not an uncommon procedure in battles of this period. One should remember that David adopted the same practice in his defeat of Goliath, which the Philistines had probably not forgotten (cf. I Sam. 17:51). The armor of Saul was placed in the house of their idols, a practice designed to encourage the faith of people with regard to the strength of their gods. Remember that the Ark of the Covenant was placed in the house of Dagon as a war trophy (cf. I Sam. 5:1-12). Notice also that David had taken the armor of Goliath and placed it in Jerusalem (v. 54). Later on the sword of Goliath was found in the sanctuary at Nob near the ephod (cf. I Sam. 21:9). It might well be that the Lord's refusal to permit David to build the temple was related to these practices. Perhaps the Lord, in this way, prevented David's turning the temple into a house of war trophies following Philistine customs. The armor of Saul ended up in the "house of Ashtaroth," one of the principal fertility deities in Philistia and Canaan.

The bodies of Saul and his sons were fastened to the walls of the city of Beth-shan, approximately two miles from the bat-

Mound of Beth-shan (in background) where the body of Saul was taken by the Philistines after his death (I Sam. 31:10). Levant Photo Service

tle area. Beth-shan was a very important fortress city in the Jordan Valley to the east of Megiddo. It guarded the vale of Jezreel which led up from the Jordan to the great plain of Esdraelon. The Egyptians had great interest in this city as evidenced by discoveries at this site. During the early part of the twelfth century B.C., Ramses III attempted to re-establish the empire of his forefathers and built a frontier military post at Beth-shan and stationed a garrison there. A number of objects have been recovered at the site which are attributable to the work of Ramses III. After about 1050 B.C., it was taken over by the Philistines as evidenced by both Biblical and archaeological data. In stratum V, excavators discovered a temple in the northern part of the mound. Many feel that this might be the "house of Ashtaroth" mentioned in I Samuel 31:10.

B. *The Burial of Saul* (31:11-13)

Word reached the inhabitants of Jabesh-gilead that the Israelites were defeated and that the mutilated bodies of Saul and
his sons were hanging on the walls of Beth-shan. The men of
Jabesh-gilead had not forgotten Saul's intervention on their behalf at an earlier period of time (I Sam. 11). In addition to that,
it should be remembered that some of the inhabitants of Jabesh-
gilead were Benjamites by marriage after the great Benjaminite
War as described in the latter chapters of the book of Judges.
The valiant men of the city arose and travelled all night. They
took the bodies of Saul and his sons, burned them and buried
them in Jabesh (vv. 11-13). The parallel passage in I Chronicles
10:12 omits the fact that the bodies of these men were burned,
perhaps because the burning of the body was at times a sign of
shame (cf. Lev. 20:14; 21:9). A fast of seven days was pro-
claimed in mourning for this great champion of Israel.

While the life of Saul is a study in contrasts, and at times impossible to fully understand, there is a sense in which Saul wins
our sympathy. He was a hero in Israel and a man who was necessary for the unification and strengthening of the nation. Unfortunately, while Saul resolved military conflicts, he was unable
to care for the inner conflicts of his own soul and the spiritual
problems which he encountered throughout his life. In the classi-
cal sense, Saul could not be called a great king, but that his
achievements were many is clear from David's exquisite elegy
recorded in II Samuel 1. Whatever military and judicial victories
may have been attributed to Saul, they are overshadowed by
his tragic spiritual failures.

Chapter 9

DAVID: KING OF JUDAH
(II Samuel 1–4)

The journey which led to the throne was a long and arduous one for David. It was an experience in the agony of defeat and sorrow on one hand, but at other times the thrill of victory. David was a man of many talents. He was a musician, writer, leader and man of valor. Because of such capabilities he was eminently qualified for the highest position in Israel. The book of II Samuel continues the story of David's rise to the throne and covers his forty years of reign. The book opens with David's accession over Judah and closes just before his death.

Because of the exquisite presentation of the historical events in the book of II Samuel we know more of David than any other man in Israel's history. His deeds, innermost thoughts, and failures are there for all to examine. Complementing the narratives in Samuel are David's writings found in the book of Psalms and a parallel history recorded in the book of II Chronicles.

The book of II Samuel divides itself naturally in two sections: (1) David's rule over Judah (1:1–4:12) and (2) David's rule over all Israel (5:1–24:25). Some commentators have found it advantageous to divide the book on its spiritual content rather than historical. In this case the book would be divided as follows: (1) David's triumphs (1:1–12:31) and (2) David's troubles (13:1–24:25).

The book of II Samuel begins much as the book of I Samuel ends, on a note of sadness. The death of Saul was a tragic turn of events for the people of Israel. Their aspirations, hopes and futures appeared to have been crushed through the humiliating defeat of the Israelite armies at Gilboa. It was in such tragic circumstances that Israel's new champion made his appearance. The task of saving Israel from total destruction was one of great difficulty and complicated by many pressures. Spiritual sensitivity and imaginative leadership were the qualities that characterized David, Judah's first king. But perhaps there is another quality which should be observed in the life of David. Far too

111

often David's military valor, political genius and spiritual insights are emphasized to the exclusion of a very basic attribute of David; namely, his keen emotion. David was a man of sensitive character, and his love for his friends was not hidden. His sorrow for those whom he respected was perfectly genuine and pure. The book of II Samuel opens with one of the most eloquent expressions of sorrow, in the most genuine sense, recorded in ancient history.

I. THE LAMENTATION OF DAVID (1:1-27)

A. *The News of Saul's Death* (1:1-16)

David was still in the town of Ziklag when he received word of Saul's death (v. 1; cf. I Sam. 30). This news did not reach David until the third day of his return to Ziklag (v. 2). Upon hearing the news he rent his clothes and put earth upon his head in a public demonstration of mourning and sorrow (cf. Josh. 7: 6; I Sam. 4:12; Job 2:12). The news of Saul's death and the defeat of Israel was brought to David by a man who identified himself as an Amalekite (vv. 8, 13). The Amalekites are well known to us because they were long-standing enemies of Israel. They attacked Israel shortly after they had left the land of Egypt (Exod. 17:8-13), and during the wilderness journey they created problems for the tribes (Deut. 25:17). They evidently were not strong enough during the period of the judges to attack Israel alone, but joined in a number of coalitions against Israel (cf. Judg. 3:13; 6:3). Saul was commanded to completely destroy these peoples because of the destruction they wrought in Israel. While Saul enjoyed a major victory, he did not fully obey the command of God and thus brought upon himself God's judgment (cf. I Sam. 15:4 ff.).

The messenger who appeared to David was probably one of those who escaped the wrath of Saul. It should also be remembered that David had just recently fought the Amalekites because they had invaded the town of Ziklag and had taken David's wives captive. It is highly doubtful that this young man was among the Amalekites whom David fought. In all probability he was a mercenary soldier who had joined Saul's forces. Notice that he described himself as one who had come "out of the camp of Israel" (v. 3; cf. v. 2 "out of the camp of Saul"). Of course, it is entirely possible that the Amalekite had no official relationship to the armies of Saul at all and was merely wandering through the battlefield in an attempt to recover whatever booty he could. However, this appears unlikely in the light of the heat of the battle that took place.

According to the Amalekite's story, he "happened by chance" to come upon Mt. Gilboa and the body of Saul (v. 6). When he reached Saul, he was badly wounded and at the point of death.[68] Saul described his condition as one of great anguish or agony (v. 9, Heb. $\check{s}\bar{a}\underline{b}\bar{a}\d{s}$).[69] Realizing that Saul's condition was hopeless he followed the request of Saul and slew him, an act which Saul's armorbearer refused to do (cf. I Sam. 31:4). Presumably, Saul's wounds were so severe that there was no possible way of removing him from the battle field.

Scholars have generally questioned the veracity of the Amalekite's story. It is their view that "the Amalekite invented this, in hope of thereby obtaining the better recompence from David."[70] Those maintaining this view feel that the Amalekite saw an opportunity for political recognition.

Others, however, have attempted to harmonize the material found in I Samuel with the Amalekite's story. It is their viewpoint that the Amalekite did find Saul still alive, but mortally wounded, and brought his life to an end at Saul's request. It is clear from the punishment David assigned that he considered the Amalekite's story as being true. David's revenge upon the Amalekite was not prompted by mere hatred of the Amalekites, although in the light of his recent conflict with them this may have been a factor. The death sentence was given primarily because

---

[68]Examples of attempted suicide are rare in Scripture. There are, however, three examples: Ahithophel (II Sam. 17:23), Zimri (I Kings 16:18) and Judas (Matt. 27:5).

[69]The Hebrew noun $\check{s}b\d{s}$ occurs only here and is difficult to translate. Some suggestions are "cramp," "dizziness" or "giddiness." (See Goldman, *op. cit.*, p. 187, also Brown, Driver and Briggs, *op. cit.*, p. 990.)

[70]C. F. Keil and F. Delitzsch, *op. cit.*, p. 286. See also H. D. M. Spence, *op. cit.*, p. 445; Francis Nichol, *op. cit.*, p. 602, and Fred Young, "I and II Samuel," *The Wycliffe Bible Commentary*, Charles Pfeiffer and Everett F. Harrison, eds. (Chicago: Moody Press, 1962), p. 293.

this Amalekite had slain the Lord's "anointed" (vv. 14-16). This was a deed which David himself refused to do a number of times (cf. I Sam. 24 and 26).

B. David's Lament for Saul and Jonathan (1:17-24)

The sorrow which David expressed over the death of Saul and Jonathan was genuine. There was no pretense or superficiality in the actions of David. His recorded elegy over the fallen and the dead is one of the most eloquent in all Scripture.

> It is one of the finest odes of the Old Testament: full of lofty sentiment, and springing from deep and sanctified emotion, in which, without the slightest allusion to his own relation to the fallen king, David celebrates without envy the bravery and virtues of Saul and his son, Jonathan, and bitterly laments their loss.[71]

Another has described David's response as follows:

> David's elegy is not supremely great poetry; it "stands out as the genuine outpouring of a noble heart, a heart too great to harbour one selfish thought in this dark hour of his country's humiliation" (Kennedy).[72]

David's elegy is divided into two parts. The first section describes David's sorrow over both Saul and Jonathan, and is introduced by the expression, "How are the mighty fallen" (vv. 19-24). The second section describes David's sorrow over Jonathan alone and is also introduced by the lament, "How are the mighty fallen" (vv. 25-26). There are several expressions in this portion of Scripture which deserve special treatment because of their apparent ambiguity. Verse 18 speaks of teaching the children of Judah "the bow." The words, "the use of," do not appear in the original. Quite evidently "the bow" was popular with the people at that time, for it was recorded in the "Book of Jasher." This book was referred to as early as Joshua 10:13. It seems to have been composed of ballads accompanied by prose

---

[71]C. F. Keil and F. Delitzsch, op. cit., p. 288.
[72]S. Goldman, op. cit., p. 189.

introductions dealing with important events and great men in the early history of Israel. David also gave instruction that the news of Saul's death and the humiliation of the nation should not be told in Gath (v. 20). This expression uttered by David apparently became a proverb in later times (cf. Mic. 1:10). It should be remembered that David resided in Gath when he lived among the Philistines (cf. I Sam. 21:10, 12; 27:2-4).

Included in the poetic descriptions of this national tragedy is the following statement: ". . . for there the shield of the mighty is vilely cast away, the shield of Saul, as though he had not been anointed with oil" (v. 21, KJV). It is clear that the translators regarded this expression as referring to the anointing of Saul. In other words, he had been cast aside as though he had never been anointed king. A better interpretation, perhaps, is that Saul was likened to a shield, left in the field to rust after the battle. Shields made of metal were commonly oiled in order to be polished and protected (cf. Isa. 21:5).

That Saul had brought a degree of prosperity to the nation is clear from David's words in verse 24. The wars of Saul were many times successful and, in fact, enriched the nation of Israel (cf. I Sam. 14:47).

II. THE CROWNING OF DAVID (2:1-32)

A. *David's Rule at Hebron* (2:1-11)

1. *The Second Anointing of David* (2:1-4)

With the death of Saul, it would seem a perfectly natural thing for David to go immediately to Judah and Israel in an attempt to occupy the throne for which he had been anointed by Samuel. But such was not the spiritual character of David. He recognized that the throne of Israel came only by divine right and only in accordance to God will. Thus the second chapter of this book begins with David's inquiry regarding his move to Judah. The inquiry was, doubtless, made through the high priest, Abiathar, who was with him (I Sam. 23:9-10; 22:20; 23:1-4). The Lord's answer came immediately, and David was commanded to go to the city of Hebron in the southern hill country. Hebron is located approximately twenty miles south of Jerusalem and

Hebron, where David was first made king (II Sam. 2:1-4, 11). Levant Photo Service

between fifteen and twenty miles away from the town of Zik-lag where David was residing. It was an ideal place for the capital in Judah since it was situated near the center of the tribe. It was well protected, being located in the mountains, and it had a long sacred history. David was no stranger to this area, for on a number of occasions he was forced to hide in the caves and valleys in the Hebron vicinity as Saul attempted to capture him. David was also more recently remembered by the gifts that he sent to the elders of Hebron after his defeat of the Ama-lekites (cf. I Sam. 30:31). In obedience to the Lord's command, David and his two wives, Ahinoam the Jezreelitess and Abigail, accompanied him to Hebron. His other wife, Michal, it will be remembered, had been given to a man by the name of Phalti and at this time was living in Benjamite territory (cf. I Sam. 25:43-44). When David reached the territory of Judah, he was warmly received and recognized as the king of that territory. David's first anointing was only in the presence of his father and his brothers (I Sam. 16:13); now, however, he stood before the whole tribe of Judah and was publicly anointed (v. 4). Fol-lowing the anointing, he received word of the heroic efforts of the men of Jabesh-gilead who had rescued the mutilated bodies of Saul and his sons and had buried them.

2. *David's Message to Jabesh-gilead* (2:5-7)

The town of Jabesh-gilead is generally identified with the site known as Tell Abu-Kharaz which is located about two miles east of the Jordan River and twenty miles south of the Sea of Galilee. After hearing of the heroism of the men of Jabesh-gilead, Da-vid performed his first formal act as king, and it was indicative of his wisdom and temperament. He commended the men of Jabesh-gilead not only on their heroic deeds in rescuing the bodies of Saul and his sons, but for the fact that they had shown this kindness to the "Lord's anointed." David fully recognized the love that the peoples of Jabesh-gilead had for the king be-cause of the protection Saul had accorded the people on a pre-vious occasion (cf. I Sam. 11:1-11). David was also fully aware of the fact that if he could win the alliance of those faithful fol-lowers of Saul, he would have gone a long way in breaking down

any animosity that would build up between himself and the
followers of Saul. It should be noted, however, that David's motives were characterized by more than mere political oppor-
tunism. His act was one of genuine kindness and sincerity. In
addition to this, David may have been offered some form of protection to the city which at this stage was without royal leadership.

3. *Ish-bosheth Made King* (2:8-11)

Abner, a relation of Saul (I Sam. 14:50), attempted to maintain the dynasty of Saul by placing Saul's surviving son Ish-bosheth upon the throne. This man was brought to the city of
Mahanaim and was there established as king over the territory
of Trans-jordan. It is questionable whether Ish-bosheth had any
significant political or military influence in the larger west bank
area. The city of Mahanaim was apparently one of some importance and influence since it was chosen as the capital of that
territory. Its importance is verified by the fact that it is mentioned in Shishak's victory inscription as *Mhnn*. Shishak (Shesh-
onk I) was the founder of the Twenty-second Dynasty in Egypt,
and is well known to us in Biblical history as the one who raided
Judah in the fifth year of King Rehoboam. The fact that Abner
made one of Saul's sons king indicates that the dynastic principle
was not unknown among the Israelites at that time.

The original name of this king was most likely Esh-baal (Heb.
'ešbā 'al) according to I Chronicles 8:33; 9:39. This name literally means "man of Baal" (or perhaps "man of the Lord"). On
the basis of Ugaritic parallels some have suggested the meaning
it-ba al ("baal lives"). Because of the implication of the name
Baal as it related to the Canaanite pantheon (and probably because of the actions of this man) the name was changed to Ish-
bosheth (Heb. *'iš bōšet* which literally means "man of shame)."
In Hosea 9:10 (cf. Jer. 3:24) the word Baal is placed in parallel
with the term *bōšet*. There is no doubt that the change of the
name had reference to his personal shame in addition to the
stigma of the name Baal (cf. Ps. 35:26). That the changing of
names among the Hebrew scribes was not uncommon is evidenced by the following examples: (a) Mephibosheth (II Sam.

4:4) was substituted for Merib-baal (I Chron. 8:34; 9:40) or Meri-baal (I Chron. 9:40). (b) Jerubbesheth (II Sam. 11:21) was substituted for Jerubbaal (Judg. 6:32; 8:35).

B. *The Battle of Gibeon* (2:12-32)

Once Ish-bosheth had been declared king of the northern kingdom, it was only a matter of time before a military confrontation would occur between the two kingdoms. This took place at a little town approximately eight miles northwest of Jerusalem. The modern village located there today is known as El-Jib, situated approximately twenty-five hundred feet above sea level. The beautiful valley which surrounds this tell is very fertile and probably was the means by which the inhabitants

The "pool" at Gibeon (El-Jib). The circular stairway leads to a tunnel which is 45 feet long and led to the water room (II Sam. 2:13). Levant Photo Service

were sustained through its long history. Excavations were carried on at El-Jib for four seasons beginning in 1956. These expeditions were conducted under the leadership of James B. Pritchard. The discoveries made at this site are most helpful to the Bible student. Identification of El-Jib as ancient Gibeon was made sure by the recovery of a number of jar handles dating from the seventh century B.C. On these jar handles were a number of inscriptions including the name of the town, Gibeon. Among the important industries at ancient Gibeon was the making of wine. This has been verified by the discovery of wine vats dating to the pre-exilic period.[73] Most spectacular of all the discoveries, however, was a large shaft leading to a pool, now identified with the pool mentioned in this chapter (cf. v. 13). This pool was cut down into a solid rock and was cylindrical in shape, measuring 37 feet in diameter and 35 feet deep. At the base of this cut the excavators discovered a circular stairway which continued by means of a tunnel down another 45 feet. This ultimately led to the water room which could be used by the people at all times, but especially during those periods when the enemy was outside the walls.[74]

When the men of Abner and the men of Joab arrived at Gibeon, they sat down on opposite sides of the pool, perhaps not intending an immediate conflict, but Abner presented Joab with a challenge which is recorded in the fourteenth verse. "Let the young men now arise and play before us, and Joab said let them arise." This verse has been difficult for many to interpret in the light of the context. It is obvious that Abner and Joab were not talking about the playing of games in our sense of the term "games." The expression "play" (Heb. *śāḥaq*) has a wide variety of uses in the Old Testament. It can refer to the playing of a game or to play by means of celebration (cf. II Sam. 6:21). But the significance of the term here is clearly related to combat as the context shows. Twelve men who were selected from the

---

[73]See James B. Pritchard, "Industry and Trade at Biblical Gibeon," *The Biblical Archaeologist*, XXIII, 1 (Feb., 1960), p. 23 ff.

[74]For a further discussion of this site see James B. Pritchard, *Gibeon, Where the Sun Stood Still* (Princeton, N. J.: Princeton University Press, 1962).

tribe of Benjamin and twelve from among the servants of David gathered near the pool and combat between these two groups was initiated. The results were inconclusive and this led to a larger battle between the two armies. The concept of battle by representation was not new for this was the principle employed in the David-Goliath confrontation (I Sam. 17).

The fashion in which the twenty-four contestants fought has been a problem for commentators to handle. Up until recent years no parallels were known in the ancient Near East which could help to shed light on the nature and purpose of such an encounter. The most significant contribution to this problem was made in an article by Y. Yadin.[75] In this article he pointed out that a relief from Tell Halaf shows two men engaged in exactly this type of combat: each grasping the other's head with one hand and the other plunging a blade into the other's side. While this discovery does not explain the particular purpose of this type of encounter, it at least provides a significant parallel. It might well be that in the near future new discoveries will shed further light on the nature and purpose of this particular type of combat.

The brief battle that followed was a demonstration of the superiority of David's men. That there were not great numbers involved in the battle is clear from the fact that only twenty men were slain in David's army and 360 in the army of Israel (vv. 30-31). During the pursuit of Saul's men, Asahel chased Abner. Asahel was the brother of Joab and Abner did not want any part of a direct encounter with this young man. He recognized that if he should slay Asahel a blood feud would develop. He gave warning to Asahel to forget his pursuit, but Asahel realized that if Abner could be slain he would have removed one of David's chief enemies and the principal power behind King Ish-bosheth in the north. The confrontation could not be avoided, however, and Abner was forced to slay the brother of Joab. The expression "the fifth rib" (v. 23) is merely a reference to the abdomen of the individual (cf. 3:27; 4:6; 20:10). There is

---

[75]Y. Yadin, "Let the Young Men, I Pray Thee, Arise and Play Before Us," *Journal of the Palestine Oriental Society,* XXI, (1948), p. 110-116.

no question that while this was not a major war, it was the beginning of long hostilities between the north and the south.

III. ABNER AND DAVID (3:1-39)

A. *The Family of David* (3:1-6)

That hostilities continued between the men of Abner and the
men of Joab is evident by the opening phrase of verse 1. The
"long war" described does not refer to continual fighting, but a
continuing state of hostility between the two parties (cf. v. 6).
The list of David's sons born during his seven-and-a-half year
reign at Hebron is given in verses 2 through 5. Some of the sons
are well known to us by virtue of their subsequent actions; the
others we know only by name. Of particular interest is the fact,
however, that Absalom was the son of a foreign princess (v. 3).
This is not without interesting implications with regard to Absalom's later rebellion.

B. *Abner's Submission to David* (3:7-26)

It is rather clear that Ish-bosheth was hardly a skillful king.
He had the throne only by virtue of his relationship to the former
king. His suspicion with regard to Abner led to further conflict
in the royal court. The charge laid against Abner is recorded in
verse 7 and constituted a serious charge. The harem in the ancient Near East was considered the property of a king's successor and, therefore, taking a woman who was part of the harem of
the previous king was interpreted as a type of claim to the throne.
Abner's action (if really carried out) was clearly a violation of
royal rights and was called into question (cf. II Sam. 12:8; 16:
21; I Kings 2:22). The response of Abner to this charge was a
very strong one. He asked if he should be considered a dog (v.
8). A dog in the ancient Near East was something thoroughly
contemptible. They were chiefly found prowling around the
towns in a half-wild condition, living off offal and garbage. The
King James Version obscures the original at this point, for it
should not read "a dog's head which against Judah," which is a
translation taken from the Vulgate, but should read "a dog's
head which belongs to Judah." Ish-bosheth was clearly not in a
position to challenge the power of Abner. This is made clear in

verse 11 and indicates that Ish-bosheth was extremely weak. He had no real power apart from Abner and his men. Abner concluded that the future of the northern kingdom was rather dark under the leadership of such an incompetent monarch and decided to change his allegiance from Ish-bosheth to David. This was initiated by sending messengers to David with the proposition that a league be formed between his men and the men of David. To this David agreed, with one condition; namely, that his wife, Michal, should be returned to him (v. 13). This led to a personal meeting between Abner and David along with the elders of Israel (vv. 17-21). When Joab heard of the private meeting, he was less than enthusiastic, for he regarded Abner as the archenemy to David's throne and could see nothing in such a meeting except an attempt to deceive (vv. 22-26).

C. *The Murder of Abner* (3:27-39)

When Abner returned to Hebron to solidify the political agreements, he was met by Joab who took him aside and slew him (v. 27). Joab was quite clearly interested in revenge for the slaying of Asahel, his brother. He may also have been considering the protection of David (cf. v. 25). More likely, however, Joab was also thinking of the future. At that time he was general of the armies of Judah. If Abner were accepted by David as an ally, his military position might be in danger. Therefore, his deed was, in fact, a protection of his own military prestige. The murder of Abner put David into a very embarrassing situation, for it would appear to the elders in the north that the whole plot had been conceived by David to eliminate his enemy. To prevent this type of rumor from developing, David immediately issued a public denouncement of the crime and denied any personal participation in the murder. The strong curse uttered by David in verse 29 indicates that he did not consider the act as justified. It should be remembered that Abner had slain Asahel in battle unwillingly and in self-defense. It should also be noted that Hebron was a city of refuge (Josh. 21:13) and in such a city not even the avenger of blood might slay the murderer without a trial (cf. Num. 35:22-25). Thus Joab violated basic laws established within Israel. The public mourning of

David and his genuine sorrow were quite impressive to the people (cf. vv. 32-36). The people in the north as well as the south recognized that David was genuinely sorry for the unnecessary death of Abner and they were pleased at the response of the king. It indicated that it was not David's desire to secure a kingdom by means of intrigue or murder.

IV. THE ASSASSINATION OF ISH-BOSHETH (4:1-12)

A. *The Assassination Described* (4:1-8)

With the death of Abner the hands of Ish-bosheth were "feeble" (Heb. "were slackened"). Without Abner, Ish-bosheth had no real support for the throne. It is probable that Ish-bosheth was unpopular with many of his own countrymen. They must have been frustrated by the inability of Ish-bosheth to strengthen and expand their government. This led to his assassination at the hands of two men. They entered his house at noontime while he rested from the heat of the day and smote him. Following this, they took his head and brought it to David to prove the success of the assassination plot. They, perhaps like the Amalekite of Chapter 1, thought that such an act would secure political favor in the eyes of David. But these men, like the Amalekite, had miscalculated the character of David. He considered the throne a sacred office not to be secured by murder and bloodshed. David was thoroughly convinced that God had promised him the throne of Israel and that in due time that throne would be his. The two murderers were judged by David and found guilty of murder. As a result, they were condemned to death (vv. 10-12) and their bodies were hung over a pool in Hebron as a public denouncement of their deeds (v. 12; cf. Deut. 21:22). Ish-bosheth was buried with full military honors in the sepulchre of Abner.

One cannot help but be impressed with the ethical and political sophistication that David brought to Israel's politics. This was in contrast to the approach adopted by King Saul. David did not follow the philosophy that the end justifies any means. He was convinced of the providential and sovereign control of his God. He believed that in the proper time the way would be open for the unification of the land and the establishment of one throne.

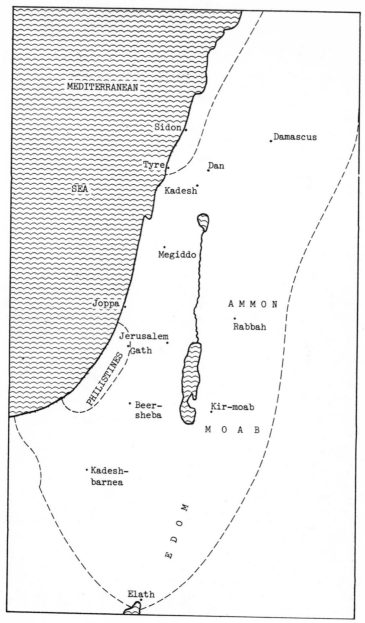

The Empire of David and Solomon

Chapter 10

ONE KING . . . ONE KINGDOM
(II Samuel 5—10)

After seven-and-one-half years of division and failure, it became apparent that the nation of Israel could not afford the luxury of such division any more. David, who had long been recognized as a champion of Israelite causes, had already proven himself a worthy king in Judah. The inability of Ish-bosheth to strengthen the northern tribes, the continued success of the Philistines in warfare and the humiliating defeat suffered by Abner's men at Gibeon made it clear that the only practical solution to their problems was to recognize David as king over all the land. Thus, with the third anointing of David, the kingdom was united and on the way to firm establishment. The decision of the elders was fully vindicated, for in less than five years David was able to bring strength and unity to a nation that was badly divided. In addition to that, he created a strong capital at Jerusalem and quickly achieved international recognition for the sovereignty of Israel. David's efforts were so successful that a really serious foreign threat did not occur until after the reign of Solomon. The same skill and prudence which characterized the boyhood days of David (cf. I Sam. 16:18; 18:5, 14, 30) now brought success to him as king.

The story of David is one of the most intriguing found anywhere. This account of unparalleled success should not be attributed to mere human wisdom, prudence, and military genius. The real key to David's rise to power was the fact that God's hand was upon him. When he was first anointed by Samuel, he was only a shepherd boy, caring for a few sheep in the hills of Bethlehem. In the chapters before us we now see David on the royal throne in Jerusalem caring for the whole flock of Israel.

I. THE LAND UNITED (5:1-25)

A. *David Anointed King over Israel* (5:1-5)

Following the disastrous reign of Ish-bosheth, the elders of the

tribes to the north were left with no real alternative but to recognize the royal authority of David. The fact of the matter is
that from a military point of view their very survival depended
on such a decision. The appearance of a large group of repre-
sentatives from the north in Hebron must have been impressive.
Included in the great numbers were elders and many warriors
(cf. v. 3 and I Chron. 12:23-40). The elders cited three reasons
why the land should be unified. First, they recognized that David had been divinely appointed as king over Israel (v. 2). Second, they reminded David of their common heritage (v. 1; cf.
Gen. 29:14; Judg. 9:2; II Sam. 19:12). Finally, they recognized
the fact that David had played an important role in Israel's military history (v. 2). The nature of kingship as viewed by the elders is instructive. They were not concerned with military needs
alone. Appropriately, David was considered a shepherd for they
requested that he should "feed" the people, Israel (Heb. *tir 'eh*
— "thou shalt pasture"; cf. 7:7). Like Saul (I Sam. 9:16; 10:1)
and Solomon (I Chron. 29:22), David was to be a "captain"
(Heb. *nāgîd*) over the nation of Israel. The former expression
probably referred to the larger realm of civil responsibility;
whereas, the latter term had reference primarily to military affairs. The third anointing of David came when he was thirty
years old, and, according to verse 4, he reigned for a period of
forty years. It is clear that the number forty is a rounded figure
of his total reign; however, the information supplied in verse 5
indicates that the reign of David extended for a short time over
forty years (cf. 2:11; I Chron. 3:4 with I Chron. 29:27).

B. *The Capture of Jerusalem* (5:6-8)

Once David was recognized as king over all the tribes, it was
inappropriate that his throne should remain in Hebron which
was centrally located in the tribe of Judah, but certainly not easily accessible to the northern tribes. David had to look for a suit-
able location which would not give political advantage to either
the north or the south. The two factions would be very sensitive
to the location of the new capital with regard to this point. David selected the city of Jerusalem which was near the border of
Judah and Benjamin. His selection was a wise one because Je-

rusalem had not been an Israelite city up to this time. It had been able to maintain its independent status under the rule of the Jebusites (cf. Josh. 15:63). Judah was successful in defeating the Jebusites on one occasion, but was not able to occupy or control the site permanently (Judg. 1:8-9). The Benjamites were also unsuccessful in an attempt to take the city on a permanent basis (cf. Judg. 1:21 with 19:11-12). In the fourteenth century B.C. the city of Jerusalem was closely aligned with Egypt and apparently depended on Egypt for help in its defense. Now that Egypt was weak, the defense of the city rested on the Jebusites alone.

Jerusalem was also an attractive selection as a capital because of its position in the high lands, which made it easy to defend. Because it is approximately 2500 feet above sea level it is a very comfortable place in which to live. The Jebusites who controlled the city were the descendants of the third son of Canaan (cf. Gen. 10:16; I Chron. 1:14). These Canaanite peoples evidently had dwelt in the hills ever since the time of Moses (cf. Num. 13:29; Josh. 11:3) and, in particular, in the Jerusalem area (Josh. 15:8; 18:16).

The Jebusites were very confident about their ability to defend the city. After all, they had successfully maintained control of Jerusalem ever since the days of Joshua. Why, then, should they fear the Israelite armies at this point? Their challenge to David indicates they were rather arrogant regarding their ability to hold the site. In effect, they told David that the city could be defended by the lame and the blind and he would still be unable to occupy it (v. 6). The particular significance of the expression "blind and lame" has been subject to a number of viewpoints on the part of commentators. J. Sidlow Baxter, apparently following some Rabbinic traditions, argues that the "lame and the blind" were actually Jebusite gods.[76] This interpretation appears rather doubtful, however. It is not likely that the Jebusites would refer to their deities as "lame and blind." Furthermore, if they were referring to gods, why did they not specifically say that? The preferred interpretation of this phrase is that:

---

[76]*Op. cit.*, p. 214.

The Jebusites relied upon the unusual natural advantages of their citadel, which stood upon Mt. Zion, the mountain shut in by deep valleys on three different sides; so in their haughty self-security they imagined that they did not even need to employ healthy and powerful warriors to resist the attack made by David, but that the blind and lame would suffice.[77]

The particular method employed by Joab in capturing the city is not made entirely clear from the terms used in verse 8. David suggested that men should enter the city by means of the "gutter" (Heb. *ṣinnôr*). The precise meaning of this word is a problem. The only other occurrence of the term in the Old Testament is in Psalm 42:7 where it is translated "water spout" (A.V.) and "water falls" (ASV.). Most commentators interpret this as a water conduit or a water course which went under the walls into the Jebusite city. On the basis of cognate parallels William F. Albright suggests that the word should be translated "hooks" or "scaling hook,"[78] but this view has not gained wide acceptance.

From the book of Chronicles it is clear that it was actually Joab who took the city and defeated the Jebusites (I Chron. 11:6). Evidently Joab and some of his men entered the city secretly by means of the water conduit, a tactic which the Jebusites had evidently not considered. In any event, the project was a success and in a very brief period of time David had complete control of the city.

C. *The Capital Established* (5:9-25)

After gaining control of the city, David immediately took steps to refortify it to guarantee its future protection. This was done by rebuilding "Millo" and sections inside the city (v. 9). The particular meaning of "Millo" is not completely known. It almost always occurs with the article. It was apparently an important part of the fortification of the stronghold of the city, perhaps that section which protected the most vulnerable part of the city

---

[77]Keil and Delitzsch, *op. cit.*, p. 315. Cf. also Francis Nichol, *op. cit.*, p. 620.

[78]"The Old Testament and Archaeology," *Old Testament Commentary*, H. C. Alleman and E. E. Flack, eds. (Philadelphia: 1954), p. 149.

in the north. Both Solomon (I Kings 11:27) and Hezekiah (II Chron. 32:5) recognized the importance of this fortress and took steps to strengthen it.

The selection of Jerusalem as the new capital was a political move of sheer genius on David's part. Its neutrality would make it attractive to the tribes in the north as well as the tribes in the south. Even more significant is the fact that David could defeat the Jebusites who had controlled the city for almost four hundred years. This certainly demonstrated his ability to achieve military goals. The results of this victory was a decided boost to David's popularity (v. 10). International recognition of David's throne came very quickly. To the northwest Hiram, king of Tyre, sent messengers to David and offered cedars, carpenters and masons to build a palace for the new king. The use of cedar in royal palaces was greatly desired by ancient Near Eastern monarchs. This is evidenced from the abundance of Egyptian literature which refers to certain ships going to Byblos to acquire that very kind of wood. The offer of Hiram not only had political implications, but economic as well. The Phoenicians had a lot to gain by establishing trade with Israel. They could supply lumber and goods from the western Mediterranean world. The tribes of Israel could provide most types of grain and food stuffs. Thus, a very significant friendship was established, one which was continued into the reign of Solomon (I Kings 5:1; 6:1, 38; 7:1; 9:10-14; II Chron. 2:3). David's prosperity in Jerusalem was not only evident in his ability to establish long-term political and economical contacts with the Phoenicians, but also in his multiplication of wives (vv. 13-16). A large harem was always a sign of wealth and prestige among ancient monarchs. However, he did so in violation of clear Biblical commands with regard to Israel's king (cf. Deut. 17:17). While polygamous practices are not condemned at this point, they are indirectly judged in the troubles that arise later in the royal court.

D. *The Capital Protected* (5:17-25)

1. *The Reason for the Philistine Attack* (5:17)

There is some doubt among scholars as to the precise chronology of events described in these verses. Many feel that the Philistine battle herein described occurred before the capture of Jerusalem. Others argue that the events were very closely related and the Philistine war occurred immediately after David's enthronement in the city. In any event, it is significant that the Philistines decided to move against David at this point. Quite evidently David's previous enthronement at Hebron was not considered a serious threat to Philistine interest. The nation of Israel was badly divided and anarchy characterized political trends in the north. But when David was recognized as king over all the land, and unification was secure, the Philistines were made aware of the fact that their success in the highlands was perhaps coming to an end. They, therefore, decided to attack immediately to prevent Israel from further uniting their military forces.

2. *The Battle Described* (5:18-24)

The attack of the Philistines occurred in two phases. The first is described in verses 18 through 21. Their original plan was to approach Jerusalem from the southwest through the valley of Rephaim (cf. Isa. 17:5). Notice that David immediately asked divine help. The habits David had formed as a young soldier now played an important role in his life as king. The Lord's answer was affirmative with the guarantee of victory (v. 19). David met them at Baal-perazim and there defeated them. The encounter was an overwhelming victory for David and his men for the Philistines were so badly routed that they even left their images behind to be burned (v. 21).[79] The second attack started from the same location (v. 22). This time David was instructed by the Lord to use a well-known tactic of outflanking the enemy. He was commanded to send a group of men behind the enemy, thereby permitting them to be attacked on all sides (vv. 23-25). Again, the effort was a complete success for David. The Philistines were routed from Geba to Gezer (v. 25).[80]

[79]The Hebrew word for "images" is *'āṣāḇ* ("idol," cf. I Sam. 31:9). In the parallel passage the term used in *'eloh'm* (I Chron. 14:12).

[80]The text of verse 25 reads Geba, but this is generally regarded as a scribal error, for both the LXX and I Chron. 14:16 read Gibeon. The location of Gibeon (northwest of Jerusalem) also favors this latter reading.

Wilderness of Judah. Levant Photo Service

3. *The Importance of the Victory*

David's victory over the Philistines at this stage was significant for several reasons. It indicated that the capital had been fully established and Israel was now a force with which to be reckoned. The victory certainly must have produced a great deal of confidence in the people regarding David's ability. Finally, this was an encouragement to David and a stablizing factor among his officials.

II. A NEW HOME FOR THE ARK (6:1-23)

A. *An Incomplete Journey* (6:1-11; cf. I Chron. 13—16)

David planned that Jerusalem should not only be the political center of the kingdom, but the religious as well. In order to establish Jerusalem as the spiritual center of Israelite life, the

presence of the Ark was needed. The Ark, at this time, was located in the town of Baale of Judah (v. 2), which is another
name for the city of Kirjath-jearim (Josh. 15:9; I Chron. 13:6).
Evidently the Ark had remained at Kirjath-jearim ever since the
day of its return from the Philistines after the death of Eli (I
Sam. 7:1). With the destruction of Shiloh by the Philistines and
the death of the priests located at Nob, Kirjath-jearim apparently was the best suited location for the Ark during these troubled
years. One writer has suggested that the Ark was, in effect, under Philistine suzerainty during this time. The following discussion is interesting although not conclusive:

> We know that Kirjath-jearim was a member of the Gibeonite
> league (Josh. 9:17) and therefore a predominantly Amorite or
> Canaanite city; and it is probable therefore that it remained
> under Philistine suzerainty, although not situated in Philistine
> territory, even when Saul had succeeded in a large measure
> throwing off the Philistine yoke. . . . Its ultimate recovery stands
> in close connection with David's repeated victories over the
> Philistines.[81]

Before the Ark was brought to Jerusalem, David's plan was
discussed with the leaders of Israel (cf. I Chron. 13:1-4). He
evidently had their complete consent before initiating this important project. Unfortunately, while David sought general counsel on moving the Ark, he failed to take care in the method
employed in its removal. The Ark was placed on a "new cart"
(v. 3) and brought out of the house of Abinadab which was located on a hill.[82] According to the law, the Ark was to be carried by the sons of Kohath (Num. 4:4-15; 7:9), and not borne
on a cart or other vehicle (Exod. 25:14-15; Num. 4:5-8). It will
be remembered that the Philistines returned the Ark on a new
cart; but this, of course, was an entirely different situation (cf. I
Sam. 6:7-14). Everything went well for David until the cart
reached the rough, rocky threshing floor of Nachon. As the Ark

---

[81]S. Goldman, *op. cit.*, p. 220.
[82]The Hebrew word *gb'h* should probably be translated here rather than
made a proper name. The word means "hill" and is so translated elsewhere
(Gen. 49:26; Exod. 17:9, etc.).

shook upon the cart, Uzzah put his hand on it to steady it, which
was a serious violation of the law (Num. 4:15). It was clear that
only the priest and the descendants of Aaron were permitted to
handle the Ark. The violation here was similar to that which was
recorded at Beth-shemesh (I Sam. 6:19). As a result of this,
Uzzah was slain by God and the failure of David's plan brought
anger to him (v. 8). Remembering the tragedy at Beth-shemesh,
David would not move the Ark any further, but placed it in the
house of Obed-edom, the Gittite, who was a Levite of the family
of Korah and later one of the door keepers of the Ark (cf. I
Chron. 15:18-24; 26:4 ff.).

B. *The Triumphal March* (6:12-23)

After a delay of three months David returned to the house of
Obed-edom to secure the Ark and attempt to take it to Jerusalem.
The Ark was moved only six paces in order to be sure that all
was in accordance with the Lord's will. Following this, a sacrifice was given to God in thanksgiving (v. 13). The removal of
the Ark to Jerusalem was no small affair in the eyes of David.
He was overwhelmed with emotion as he thought of the spiritual
and practical implications of its presence in Jerusalem. The evidence of his joy is witnessed in the fact that he "danced" before
the Lord with all his might. The Hebrew word for "danced" is
mekarkēr which literally means to "whirl" or to "whirl around."
While the occasion was a thrilling one for David, it was somewhat less than that for David's wife, Michal. When she saw
David leaping and dancing before the Lord, she viewed this as
a despicable act in the eyes of the public (v. 16). It is interesting to note that the historian identified her as "Saul's daughter"
rather than the wife of David. Perhaps her actions and attitude
in this situation were more characteristic of her father than of
her husband. She may have objected to David's actions because
it was more common for the women to act this way than for the
men (cf. Exod. 15:20-21; Judg. 11:34; I Sam. 18:6). Her displeasure, however, was more likely tied in with her insensitivity
to the religious significance of this occasion. Her speeches to
David were characterized by sarcasm and bitterness (cf. v. 20).
This brought a quick and decisive response from David in which

he pointed out that he had no intention of changing his behavior purely on her behalf. He planned to continue to "play"
before the Lord,[83] and "be more vile than thus" (better translated "I will be more lightly esteemed than this"). As a result of
this estrangement, Michal had no children until the day of her
death (v. 23; cf. 20:3; I Chron. 15:29).

III. THE KING'S DESIRE (7:1-29)

A. *David's Proposal and God's Response* (7:1-17)

Only one thing troubled David as he viewed the situation in
Jerusalem after the Ark had been placed there. The Phoenicians
had built him a beautiful palace of cedar, but the dwelling place
of the Ark was quite unimpressive (vv. 1-2). It was David's desire that the Ark should rest in a temple worthy of its importance. In order to ascertain God's will in this matter, he consulted with Nathan, the prophet (vv. 2-3). While this is the first
mention of Nathan, he, in all probability, had an important role
in the court of David prior to this time, most likely in the capacity of an advisor. Later he figured prominently in the story of
Bathsheba (II Sam. 12:1 ff.) and in the determination of succes-
sion to the throne (I Kings 1:11 ff.). According to I Chronicles
29:29 he, along with Gad, was one of the chroniclers of David's
reign (cf. II Chron. 9:29). The answer that Nathan gave was
affirmative, but quite clearly too hasty. Nathan judged the arguments of David and considered them to be valid. That evening
the Lord spoke to Nathan and instructed him to return to David
with a negative answer, thus, not permitting him to construct
the temple at that time.

By studying this context, along with other passages, one is able
to discover at least four reasons why David's request was rejected: (1) A historical argument (v. 6). A sophisticated temple
had not been required up to this point, so why now? (2) Had
God asked for this (v. 7)? In other words, the request did not
come from the Lord, but from David alone. (3) He was not
permitted to build this temple because he had ". . . shed much

---

[83]The Hebrew is *sihaqti* from *sahaq*. This is the same word used in 2:14.

blood upon the earth" (I Chron. 22:8; 28:3). His many years as a warrior involved him in the bloodshed of hundreds and therefore made his candidacy inappropriate for such an important task. It is also possible that under David the temple might become a treasure house of war trophies (cf. I Sam. 17:54 with 21:9). This was a common practice among the Philistines in whose land he had dwelt for over a year (I Sam. 5). (4) It was too soon to build the temple. David's judgment as to the security of the city was evidently inaccurate. It is clear from I Kings 5:3-4 that the destruction of the city was indeed possible at this time in David's life.

Nathan's conversation with the king on the next day must have been a very difficult one for him. God's response was not wholly negative, however, for David was reminded of the fact that he was the recipient of a sovereign call (v. 8) and had survived to this day because of divine protection (v. 9). In this he found encouragement (v. 10). While David would not be permitted to build a house for the Ark, the Lord promised him that a greater house would be built which would be established forever (v. 13). The Davidic covenant was a very important affirmation of God's intention to complete that which he had promised to Abraham (Gen. 12). This covenant consisted of three essential elements: (1) a posterity (vv. 12, 13, 16), (2) a throne (vv. 13, 16; cf. Luke 1:32) and (3) a kingdom (vv. 13, 16; cf. Luke 1:33). The nature and scope of this covenant are such that their fulfillment could not have been realized in the days of Solomon, but will find their ultimate fulfillment in Christ through the establishment of His kingdom on earth (cf. Isa. 9:6).

C. *Worship and Praise* (7:18-29)

The response of David is an exquisite example of true submission to God's will. Rather than mourning the loss of his well-conceived plans, David rejoiced in the promise of future blessing. In this section of the chapter David recognized the sovereignty of his Lord and the right of God to change his plans. David was also thoroughly convinced of the perfection with which God controls the affairs of men. The whole history of Israel up to this point was an evidence of God's inerrant working among His people (cf. v. 23 ff.). The attitude expressed by David should be that which characterizes all believers as God's will is clearly revealed. In the light of such humiliation, it is not difficult to see why God called David "a man after His own heart."

IV. A SUMMARY OF DAVID'S WARS (8:1-18)

While the wars of Saul were characteristically defensive in nature, the wars of David took on the character of being offensive and led to expansion of the borders of Israel. The chapter before us describes the successful campaigns of David as they related to the surrounding nations. It is evident that David took geography and natural resources into consideration as he planned the expansion of Israel's borders.

A. *The Defeat of Philistia and Moab* (8:1-2)

It is not surprising that David waged campaigns against the Philistines who were at this time Israel's most bitter enemies. He was successful in subduing them and confining their military activity to a small area. In addition, he took the town of Metheg-ammah which translated means "bridle of the mother city." This was another name for the city of Gath, which was one of the principal towns of the Philistine pentapolis (I Chron. 18:1).

The fact that David conducted a campaign against Moab indicates a change of attitude on his part concerning these people. He had previously enjoyed rather good relations with Moab as indicated by their willingness to provide asylum for David's parents when he was a fugitive from Saul (cf. I Sam. 22:3-4). The reason for David's change of attitude has been attributed to a deception on the part of the Moabites resulting in the death of David's parents; however, this tradition cannot be verified. According to verse 2 only one-third of the captives were permitted to live after David's victory.[84]

B. *Victory over the Arameans* (8:3-12)

Having subjected the Philistines to the west and the Moabites

---

[84]Cf. J. Davis, *Biblical Numerology*, p. 82.

to the east, David turned his attention to the north and the kingdom of the Arameans. One of the key areas was the kingdom of
Zobah, a small territory west of the Euphrates and northeast of
the city of Damascus. David's victory over King Hadadezer
helped to secure the northern borders of Israel and to provide a
buffer zone from enemies further north. David's efforts in that
area were very successful, leading to the capture of many horses
and chariots (v. 4). David "houghed" the chariot horses; that is,
the horses were disabled by cutting the back sinews of their
hind legs. This rendered the animals unfit for use in war (cf.
Josh. 11:6-9). David did, however, keep a hundred chariots out
of this booty (v. 4). To guarantee protection for the northern
borders of his kingdom he established garrisons near Damascus.
Notice that after these victories David brought the shields of
gold that were taken from the servants of Hadadezer and brought
them to Jerusalem. Could it be that these were taken as war
trophies? It is not impossible to conceive that among the interests of David in building a temple was to provide a place to store
trophies such as these.

C. *The Defeat of Edom* (8:13-14)

The Hebrew text indicates that David fought "Arameans in
the valley of salt" (v. 13). It is highly doubtful, however, that
the term Aramean is the correct one. The text of verse 13 appears to have suffered from a copyist error. On this point almost
all commentators are agreed. According to I Chronicles 18:12,
the title of Psalm 40, and the immediate context of this chapter,
Edom, not Syria, was the enemy defeated in the valley of salt.
The geographic proximity of the valley of salt to Edom is clearly
seen in II Kings 14:7. In the light of the foregoing evidence,
most scholars feel that the text should read Edomites rather than
Arameans. A careful study of the Hebrew letters indicates a
confusion of *dalet* and *resh* by the scribes. David's victory over
the Edomites in the territory south of the Dead Sea was important because it gave David access to the very rich copper
mines of the Arabah. Furthermore, it placed control of important
trade routes from the gulf of Aqaba in David's hands.

D. *David's Court Officials* (8:15-18)

In addition to being a skillful warrior and a good leader, David was a successful organizer as evidenced by this portion of the text. The military organization was headed up by Joab, the son of Zeruiah (v. 16). The scribal organization within the royal court included a "recorder" (Heb. *mazkîr* — "rememberer") and a "scribe" (Heb. *sōpēr*). The particular functions of a recorder and the scribe apparently were different and most likely were parallel to similar Egyptian offices. Other texts indicate that the recorder was an important individual in the royal court (cf. II Kings 18:18-37; II Chron. 34:8; Esth. 6:1). According to verse 17 David had two priests over the land, Zadok and Ahimelech. The appointment of Ahimelech as one of the priests is interesting, for he was the son of Abiathar, the only one to escape Saul's senseless massacre of the priests of Nob (cf. I Sam. 22:11-20). Some scholars have felt that the appointment of Ahimelech to the high priesthood was to repay a debt to him or to salve a troubled conscience over the lie that caused the slaughter; however, this is not so indicated in the text. The personal bodyguard of the king was made up of two groups of men known as the Cherethites and Pelethites (v. 18; cf. 15:18; 20:7; 23; I Kings 1:38, 44; I Chron. 18:17). The Cherethites were many times associated with the Philistines and may have been part of that nation (I Sam. 30:14 cf. Ezek. 25:16; Zeph. 2:5).

V. DAVID AND MEPHIBOSHETH (9:1-13)

David's kindness to this surviving son of Jonathan is significant. This move on his part was prompted by two things: (1) The covenant which he had made with Jonathan, and (2) the attempt to end any conflict between his household and the household of Saul. The events described in this chapter probably took place about fourteen years after the death of Jonathan since Mephibosheth was then five years old (4:4) and now had a young son (v. 12). The kindness of David was genuine, however. It was a "kindness of God" (v. 3). Mephibosheth apparently was no threat to the throne of David, for he was lame in both feet (vv. 3, 13). Mephibosheth was brought to the royal court of David and there given food and shelter (v. 11).

VI. THE AMMONITE-SYRIAN WAR (10:1-19)

When David was a fugitive, he evidently was able to find asylum and protection among the Ammonites under Nahash (v. 2). When Nahash died, his son took the throne. David attempted to secure peaceful relations with him, but the advisors of the king interpreted this as an attempt to spy out the city and to ultimately overthrow it (v. 3). David's men were humiliated by having half their beards cut and half the garments cut away. The shame was so great that they were not able to return to Jerusalem until their beards had grown back (v. 5). The Ammonites were really in no position to encounter David in warfare by themselves, so they "hired" Arameans from the north from the kingdoms of Bethrehob and Zoba. According to I Chronicles 19:6 Hanun, king of the Ammonites, paid one thousand talents of silver to hire horsemen and chariots which gives some indication of the crucial nature of the upcoming battle.

The first encounter with Joab and the troops of Israel ended in defeat for the Ammonite-Aramean coalition. Joab, by skillfully using his troops, was able to outflank them and defeat them. The Arameans no longer viewed the situation from the standpoint of mere professional obligation, for the security of their towns was now at stake. A second encounter followed which is described in verses 15 through the end of the chapter. Again Joab and his men were victorious over the Arameans as they marched down from the north. This victory completely humiliated the Ammonites and brought peace with the Arameans to the north (v. 19). Thus, David had secured all of the borders of Israel and expanded them so that the empire had now reached the greatest height of his career.

Chapter 11

SHAME AND SORROW
(II Samuel 11–14)

The greatest victories are sometimes annulled by foolish mistakes. David's unparalleled success had made it possible for him to enjoy all the comforts of royal life. No longer did he need to be in the field of combat since capable leadership was provided by Joab and there were no more immediate serious threats to the kingdom. It was in these circumstances that David's greatest failure occurred (cf. I Kings 15:5). It was tragic indeed that such a brilliant career should be marred in this manner; however, it is well known that Satan is most effective in his approaches when the believer is comfortable and successful.

I. DAVID'S SIN WITH BATH-SHEBA (11:1–12:31)

A. *The Occasion of the Sin* (11:1)

That David was free from military responsibility because of his previous successes is made clear in the first verse of this chapter. Under David's leadership the armies of Israel had soundly defeated the Ammonite-Syrian coalition (10:13-19). When David left the battlefield, the victory was clearly Israel's. The only operation that remained was the final conquest of the capital city of the Ammonites, Rabbah (11:1). The information provided in verse 1 indicates that the time when David committed this sin was the spring of the year. The Authorized Version implies that this event took place "after the year was expired," but this is a poor translation of the original. A better rendering would be "after the return of the year" (Heb. *litšûbat haššānāh*). The precise meaning of this expression is made even clearer by the next clause which states that this was the time of the year "when kings go forth to battle."[85] It was during the spring that armies normally conducted their campaigns because

---

[85]For another view on this problem, see S. Goldman, *op. cit.*, pp. 243-244.

of the favorable weather and the availability of food (cf. I Kings 20:22, 26). The winter season was cold and wet, thus making many roads impassable.

While the main armies of Israel surrounded the city of Rabbah, smaller army units were sent throughout the land and they "wasted the country of the children of Ammon" (I Chron. 20:1). "After the custom of ancient warfare, while the army was besieging Rabbah, foraging parties were sent out to lay waste the country and cut off any stragglers. Cf. I Sam. 13:17-18."[86]

B. *The Sequence of Sin* (11:2-5)

It was toward evening, following David's afternoon rest, that he saw Bath-sheba washing herself and found her very attractive. David's palace was situated high on Mount Ophel which gave him a view over the many homes which were built along the slopes of that mountain. It was during these moments of idleness and inactivity that David was most severely tempted by Satan. One has well summarized the situation in this way:

> Satan chose this moment to bring upon the king of Israel a temptation that was to cause him deep humiliation and disgrace. David tragically forgot that there was an enemy greater than men. Feeling himself strong and secure against his earthly enemies, intoxicated by his prosperity and success, while receiving the plaudits of men, Israel's honored hero and saint was thrown off his guard. Inperceptibly the inner defenses of his soul had weakened, until he yielded to a temptation that transformed him into a shameless sinner.[87]

The sequence of David's sin is most instructive. There are three key verbs which describe the process by which David was led into adultery. According to verse 2 he *saw* a woman washing herself. The next step was *inquiry* (v. 3) by which he discovered not only the name of the woman, but also the fact that she was married to Uriah the Hittite. The third step, recorded

[86]F. Gardner, "II Samuel," *Ellicott's Commentary on the Whole Bible* (Grand Rapids: Zondervan Publishing House, n.d.), II, p. 471.

[87]Francis Nichol, ed. *op. cit.*, p. 646.

in verse 4, was his *participation* in sin. The sequence of sin described in these verses is not new. Looking back to the garden of Eden one can see a similar sequence described. In Genesis 3:6 we are told that Eve "saw" that the tree was good for food and she "*desired*" to have a portion. Finally she "*took*" of the fruit. This sin was not consummated in seclusion, for Adam later became involved (Gen. 3:6). The result was the loss of purity, glory, and fellowship with God (Gen. 3:7). The same sequence is also attested in the story of Achan recorded in Joshua 7. Achan, we are told, "*saw*" the various objects in the destroyed city of Jericho. He found these very attractive and "*coveted them*" and then "*took*" them (Josh. 7:21). This, of course, led to disaster and death for him and for the members of his family. In the light of the above examples of temptation, failure and sin, one is reminded of the admonition of James that "when lust has conceived it bringeth forth sin" (James 1:15). David's sin was not one of ignorance, for having inquired as to the identity of the young lady, he was informed that she was the wife of Uriah, one of David's best soldiers (cf. II Sam. 23:39). The fact that David knew that Bath-sheba was married made this sin even greater. Verse 4 indicates that David sent messengers to take Bath-sheba. Commentators are not sure that this was a seizure by force. Some are inclined to believe that Bath-sheba's bathing in view of the royal palace was intentional and that her actions were characterized by easy submission to all of David's commands. Others feel that Bath-sheba bathed in privacy and David's view of her was a mere accident. According to this view, she was taken by force to be part of the royal harem of the king. While Bath-sheba was obviously a woman of beauty there is some evidence that she lacked discretion on various occasions (cf. I Kings 2:13-22). In a short time it became clear that the sin could no longer be completely concealed or forgotten (v. 5). The sin that David committed was, according to law, punishable by death (cf. Lev. 20:10).

C. *The Results of Sin* (11:6-27)

Unwilling to face up to his sin and confess it, David attempted to cover up that which he had done. Through the process of deceit and evil maneuvers he attempted to make the conception look perfectly natural. The first attempt of David is recorded in verses 6 through 12. When Uriah returned from Ammonite territory he was taken to the king's palace and given gifts from the king to take home, but Uriah refused the liberty offered to him and remained at the king's house. Verse 11 gives the impression that Uriah refused the king's offer on the grounds of inequity. His fellow soldiers were out in the field suffering hardship, so why should he enjoy such luxury and ease? The second attempt of David to get Uriah home is recorded in verse 13. This time he permitted Uriah to eat with him and in the process made him drunk, but this again failed for Uriah refused to return to his home. The persistent refusal of Uriah to return home has raised suspicion in the minds of some as to whether or not Uriah had been informed of the situation.

There is no question that Uriah was a capable soldier and one of David's best. That he was a Hittite might indicate that he was hired as a mercenary soldier, a professional with outstanding skill. It is also possible, of course, that he was a proselyte to the Israelite faith.

In any event, scholars are divided as to whether or not Uriah had been informed with regard to David's relationship to Bathsheba. One writer says, "It is quite unnecessary to suppose that Uriah had any suspicion of what had been done. His conduct and language is simply that of a brave, frank, generous-hearted soldier."[88] However, it appears more likely that Uriah may have known of his wife's unfaithfulness. "Her visit to David was known to the palace servants, and it is unlikely that David's court was more discreet and less addicted to malicious gossip than royal courts have been throughout all history."[89]

The third attempt of David to cover up his sin was the resort to murder. The accomplishment of this task is described in verse 15 and following. By means of a royal letter Joab was commanded to place Uriah in the most difficult battle, so as to guarantee his death. Joab accomplished this goal by preparing an

<hr/>

[88]F. Gardner, *op. cit.*, p. 471.
[89]S. Goldman, *op. cit.*, p. 245. See also C. F. Keil and F. Delitzsch, *op. cit.*, p. 384.

attack against the city gate of Rabbah which was probably the most heavily defended part of the city (v. 23). This led to the death of Uriah. It appears that David, at this point, had lowered himself to the evil devices of his predecessor, King Saul. Saul earlier had attempted to take the life of David by similar maneuverings (I Sam. 18:25). When Bath-sheba heard of her husband's death, "she mourned" (v. 26). As to the precise nature of this sorrow, Adam Clarke observes "the whole of her conduct indicates that she observed form without feeling the power of sorrow. She lost a captain and got a king for her spouse; this must have been deep infliction indeed, and therefore . . . 'she shed reluctant tears, and forced out groans from a joyful heart.' "[90] Following the period of mourning[91] she became the wife of David (v. 27). While it might appear that the devices of David had concealed his sin before the general public, God, who is omniscient, knew of the whole affair (v. 27).

D. The Confession of Sin (12:1-25)

1. Nathan's Message (12:1-14)

The very fact that David's sin and subsequent repentance is recorded in such detail is, in itself, quite unique as viewed from the vantage point of ancient Near Eastern literature generally. The record of David's failure is perhaps one of the strongest proofs of divine inspiration of Scripture. It was not normal for scribes to record the failure of ancient Near Eastern monarchs. Furthermore, the particular ethic conveyed in these chapters is likewise unique. To the eastern mind, for a king to take the wife of a subject was quite normal and that which was within the rights of an absolute sovereign. The fact of the matter is, few kings of the ancient Near East would have taken the trouble to attempt to conceal such sin. The fact that David went to great lengths indicates that Israel was dominated by moral principles far superior to that of her neighbors. It is generally agreed that

---

[90]*Clarke's Commentary* (New York: Carlton and Phillips, 1854), II, p. 336.

[91]The usual period of mourning was seven days (cf. Gen. 50:10; I Sam. 31:13).

the appearance of Nathan before David took place approximately one year after his marriage to Bath-sheba (cf. 11:27 with 12:14-15). For David, that year was one of the most bitter and frustrating in all his life. Psalm 32 appears to be a reference to these events, and verses 3 and 4 are very vivid descriptions of the effects that concealed sin has on one's life.

a. *The method of approach* (12:1-6). Nathan's approach to David on this very difficult occasion was both skillful and effective. With the use of a parable[92] he was able to both reveal David's sin and allow David to indict himself. The illustration was an appropriate one, for David knew how attached one could become to a lamb as a pet since he had been a shepherd for a good part of his life. It is also obvious that Nathan was employing David's knowledge of the law to make his sin clear. As Nathan described the arrogance of the rich man who seized that precious new lamb from the poor man, one can imagine the indignant response of David. In effect, Nathan was describing David's seizure of Uriah's wife, who to him was precious.

b. *The application* (12:7-12). Once David had recognized the injustice involved in the parable, Nathan was then prepared to make the application to David. In very clear, concise language he told David, "Thou art the man" (v. 7). This was no easy task for Nathan who had been with David for many years. He acted here as a true prophet in the exposure of sin (cf. Mic. 3:8). As a result of David's sin the Lord had promised a twofold punishment upon him and his household. First of all, during his lifetime his house would be characterized by rebellion and sin (vv. 11-13). The second phase of divine punishment involved the death of that child born through adultery (v. 14). While some might consider the punishment given by God to have been unjust, it should be remembered that David had committed two sins both of which required the death penalty (adultery, Lev. 20:10, and murder, Lev. 24:17). Therefore, the response of God was a just and merciful one.

c. *The confession* (12:13-14). David's confession must be regarded as genuine. He made no excuses for his sin and did not

---

[92]Note the use of parables elsewhere: 14:2-11; I Kings 20:35-41.

attempt to conceal his guilt any longer. The full expression of David's confession can be studied in Psalm 51, which is an important commentary on verse 13.

The whole story of David's temptation, fall, and punishment should not be a cause for despair, but instruction in the righteousness of God and His mercy toward the sinner. David's ". . . . fall, as St. Augustine has said, should put upon their guard those who have not fallen, and save from despair those who have."[93]

2. *Death and Life* (12:15-25)

After Nathan's departure, the child born to Bath-sheba became very sick and ultimately died. David concluded the fasting period and then arose to look toward the future. There does not appear to be any bitterness in his heart; on the contrary, this tragedy led him to bend the knee in worship to his God (v. 20). David was given another son by Bath-sheba whose name is familiar to all students of the Old Testament, Solomon (vv. 24-25).

E. *The Defeat of Rabbah* (12:26-31)

This portion of the chapter resumes the narrative begun in Chapters 10 and 11 (verse 1). The material in the remaining part of Chapter 11 and the early part of Chapter 12 is therefore parenthetical. It is interesting to note that David's sin with Bath-sheba does not appear in the parallel Chronicles account. Joab was able to complete the siege of the capital city and take it. He called David to the site of Rabbah so that David might enter the city and be declared the victor over that town lest Joab receive national recognition for the victory (v. 28). The victory over this city was significant, and involved the capture of many precious objects (v. 30). Verse 31, which describes the activities of David following this victory, presents a difficult problem. The Hebrew text is not entirely clear as to the nature of David's activity. Two views have emerged regarding the interpretation of the passage. The first view considers the implements mentioned as instruments of torture and death. The latter part of

---

[93]F. Gardner, *op. cit.,* p. 471.

the verse would then be translated "he sawed them in pieces with the saw and with iron harrows." If this translation is adopted, it means that the Hebrew text needs to be changed, for presently the text literally reads *wayyāśem bammegērāh* ("and he put them under saws"). To arrive at the above translation, the expression *wayyāśem* would need to be changed so as to read *wayyāśar* (from the root *śûr*).[94] The above translation seems to be the one adopted by the writer of Chronicles (cf. I Chron. 20:3). This, in effect, means that David punished the Ammonites with bodily mutilation. Many have objected to this conclusion. As one commentator observes, "such cruelties would be in accord with the common customs of the time, but not with David's character."[95]

The other view is that the Hebrew text should remain as it presently stands in the Samuel passage and read, "and he appointed to labor with saws"; that is, the Ammonites were put to various forms of slave labor.[96]

II. AMNON AND TAMAR (13:1-39)

The events recorded in this chapter most likely took place after David's marriage with Bath-sheba and the war with the Ammonites. The events described in the following chapters relate to the history of David's court and the tragedies which followed his sin with Bath-sheba. There is no question as to the cause and effect relationship of David's sin and punishment to these events.

A. *Amnon's Crime* (13:1-22)

The story of Absalom, Tamar, and Amnon is tragic and disheartening. Unfortunately, it does not represent an event that occurred only once in history. The tragedies of this chapter have been repeated many times since the days of David. Men have refused the counsel of Scripture and thus have paid the price of sin and its immediate consequences.

According to II Samuel 3:3, Absalom and Tamar were the

---

[94]See C. F. Keil and F. Delitzsch, *op. cit.*, p. 395.
[95]Francis Nichol, *op. cit.*, p. 654.
[96]*Ibid.*

children of Maacah, daughter of Talmi, king of Geshur. Absalom, according to this verse, had been born to David in Hebron.
Amnon was the oldest son of David, by Ahinoam, the Jezreelite
(3:2).

The story that follows describes Amnon's love for Tamar, the
beautiful sister of his step-brother, Absalom. His love for her,
however, was not genuine. It involved no more than infatuation
and sensuous desire. His desires for her became so strong that
he became ill. Her upright behavior prevented an easy approach. It was through the advice of a "friend" that he was able
to deceive her and commit his sin (v. 3 ff.). When word of his
evil deed reached David, he was extremely angry, but found
himself incapable of appropriate and stern discipline. This, of
course, is understandable in the light of his own failures in the
area of moral restraint (cf. v. 21). Absalom developed a bitter
hatred for Amnon and for two years sought an occasion to take
his life (vv. 22-23).

B. *Absalom's Revenge* (13:23-39)

The hatred that Absalom had for Amnon was precipitated
mainly by Amnon's abuse of his sister; however, it is not impossible that Absalom's hatred for him also involved the fact that
Amnon was the first-born and, therefore, probably the heir to the
throne after David. When the occasion finally presented itself,
Absalom took the necessary steps to bring the life of Amnon to
an end. When David received word of this tragedy, he tore his
garments and prostrated himself to the ground in sorrow (v. 31).
The comfort offered by Jonadab was something short of genuine
consolation (vv. 32-33). Absalom, recognizing the possibility of
the king's wrath, fled from the royal court and went to Talmai,
king of Geshur (v. 37). David's mourning lasted over a long
period of time and his separation from Absalom continued for a
period of approximately three years (v. 38).

III. THE RETURN OF ABSALOM (14:1-33)

A. *Joab's Plot* (14:1-20)

Joab had great concern for the disposition of David. David's
broken heart and despondent countenance would have a disas-

Entrance to Tomb 302 at Tekoa. Used in the Iron II (900-600 B.C.) and Roman Periods. Courtesy Tekoa Archaeological Expedition

1968 Tomb Excavations at Tekoa under the supervision of the author. Courtesy Tekoa Archaeological Expedition

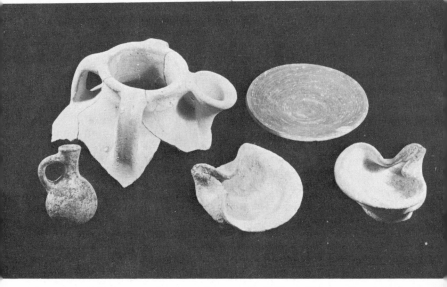

Iron Age II Pottery and Lamps from tomb 302 at Tekoa. Excavated in 1968. Courtesy Tekoa Archaeological Expedition

trous effect on the morale of both the armies and the people of Israel. He therefore took immediate steps to reconcile the two. This was once again done by the use of a parable.

In order to approach David in a subtle manner so as not to reveal his own intentions, Joab sent to Tekoa and there sought out "a wise woman." It is interesting to observe the mention of Tekoa here and in 23:26. Tekoa was a rather important site during this period of time. The city had a long history in Scripture and, of course, is most well known to us as the home town of the prophet Amos. The mound of Tekoa lies approximately five miles south of Bethlehem and for centuries has remained in ruins. It was not until 1968 when the Tekoa Archaeological Expedition first began excavations at the site that some of the history of this significant town was illuminated. It was the author's privilege to be supervisor of Field III in that expedition, which involved the excavation of the ancient tombs. In addition to work done on the churches on the top of the mound, five tombs were excavated, some of which dated back to the ninth century B.C. A fine collection of pottery indicated rather extensive occupation of the site during the days of the prophet Amos.[97]

The parable given by the wise woman was immediately recognized by David as a device of Joab to reconcile himself and Absalom (v. 19). David, however, did not appear to be greatly disturbed by the fact that Joab used this woman to convey his feelings to him.

B. *The Return and Restoration of Absalom* (14:21-33)

David recognized the effect that Absalom's separation was having on his own life. With reservation he agreed to bring Absalom back to Jerusalem again. This was done, but the restoration was somewhat incomplete. For two years Absalom did not enjoy the privilege of entering the royal court of David (cf. vv. 24, 28).

---

[97]For further information on the Tekoa excavations see Martin H. Heicksen, "Tekoa: Excavations in 1968," *Grace Journal*, X, 2 (Spring, 1969), pp. 3 ff. Also John J. Davis, "Tombs Tell Tales," *Brethren Missionary Herald*, XXXI, 10, p. 16 ff. A complete report of this work can be found in *Excavations at Tekoa, 1968*, Martin H. Heicksen (ed.) Near East Institute of Archaeology, Box 168, Wheaton, Illinois.

Mound of Tekoa, home of the "wise woman" who helped Joab (II Sam. 14:2) and Ira, one of David's "mighty men" (II Sam. 23:26). Excavations were begun here in 1968 under the Tekoa Archaeological Expedition, Martin H. Heicksen, Director. Courtesy Tekoa Archaeological Expedition

Finally, Joab stepped in again and encouraged the king to completely restore Absalom. David finally agreed to forgive Absalom of the past deed and permit him full court privileges (v. 33). What appeared to be a step toward peace later turned out to be the first step in the development of another tragedy in the royal court of David.

Chapter 12

TURMOIL IN JERUSALEM
(II Samuel 15—24)

The concluding chapters of II Samuel are filled with the misfortune that characterized the last days of David's reign. The full effects of Nathan's prophecy were now being realized (cf. II Sam. 12:1 ff.). The royal court experienced insurrection, disappointment, and sorrow. The rebellion of Absalom, and the humiliation of David described in the chapters that follow were fully anticipated in Nathan's prophecy (cf. II Sam. 12:1 ff.). It is important to observe that the prophetic statements of Nathan were not vague generalites, but were explicit and to the point. David not only experienced rebellion within his own household, but public humiliation brought by several individuals. The greatest turmoil experienced by David was not from the armies that surrounded Israel, but from the tension and anarchy from within. Some of this was due to his own failure in disciplining his sons, and much of it was due to the effects of his sin which was quite clearly a turning point in his successful career. While David enjoyed the opportunity of gathering materials for the temple and securing the borders of Israel, it was not his lot to realize the blessing of peace and tranquillity in the royal court during the last years of his reign.

I. REVOLT AND HUMILIATION (15:1–19:9)

A. *The Insurrection Planned* (15:1-12)

Not long after the restoration of Absalom to the royal court, he sought every opportunity to capture the imagination and the hearts of the people. Verse 2 informs us that he rose up early and made a daily appearance at the gate where legal business was commonly conducted. When controversy arose he consistently took the side of the oppressed and used this occasion to raise questions about the judicial capabilities of his father (v. 3). Along with this was the constant suggestion that if he were made a judge in the land, justice would be more equitable (v. 4). Thus, after a period of time Absalom had gained a rather large following, especially among those who had opposed David from the beginning.

Verse 7 is problematic in that it indicates that a period of forty years transpired before Absalom brought about the full insurrection; however, it is clear that the number forty is not the best reading of the text at this point. The Lucian edition of the Septuagint and the Syriac read "four years" instead of forty. This is the number suggested by Josephus in *Antiquities*, VII. 9.1. The point at which these four years began was probably Absalom's return to Jerusalem. If this were the case, it would mean that two of these years were spent in turning the people's hearts from David (II Sam. 14:28).[98]

In order to have freedom and to make the insurrection successful, Absalom requested permission to return to Hebron to pay a vow made some years earlier (vv. 7-8). All of this, of course, was a subtle disguise to have freedom in planning the insurrection.[99] Rebellion against the throne was very carefully prepared and executed. While at Hebron, Absalom sent spies throughout the various tribes of Israel to encourage sympathy for his cause and to organize the insurrection. The right hand man and advisor of Absalom was Ahithophel the Gilonite. This man had been David's counsellor for some years, but he evidently had never really supported the throne genuinely and this is understandable in the light of his relationship to Bath-sheba. A comparison of II Samuel 11:3 with II Samuel 23:24-39 indicates that Ahithophel was the grandfather of Bath-sheba. It is not impossible that ever since the violent death of Uriah, Ahithophel had been looking for an opportunity for revenge. With the rebellion of David's son, Absalom, his opportunity had arrived.

The insurrection of Absalom enjoyed a degree of success, at

---

[98]The Talmud reckoned the "forty years" from the time when the Israelites demanded a king. Ralbag (1288-1344) suggested the figure represented the time from the time of David's anointing by Samuel. See S. Goldman, *op. cit.*, p. 275.

[99]One is reminded of the deceit employed by Amnon to accomplish evil goals (II Sam. 13:6-7).

least for a period of time. This success is not accounted for merely on the basis of the political skill or genius of Absalom. He was free to work this deceit because of the laxness of David toward his sons in matters of discipline (I Kings 1:6). It is also possible that in those years David lacked the resolute firmness that was needed for the implementation of consistent discipline. Furthermore, there most likely was a very strong anti-Davidic feeling in Hebron. Many people in Hebron had probably not forgiven David for changing the capital from Hebron to Jerusalem and took this occasion to express their dissatisfaction at that move. It was for this reason that Absalom returned to the place of his birth. There he could be assured of a sympathetic ear.

B. *The Flight of David* (15:13–17:29)

David's response to the news of Absalom's rebellion is somewhat surprising and puzzling. Could it be that such a brilliant king would be so easily deceived by the obvious actions and intentions of his son? Duff Cooper, an English author, acutely observes that David must have refused "to listen to what he did not want to hear. He could not bear to think that his lovely, charming son might be guilty of harboring thoughts of rebellion; and when evidence to that effect was brought to him he preferred to dismiss it."[100] When David was informed of the widespread discontent with his leadership and the organized insurrection of Absalom, he fled the city, perhaps recognizing that the strength of the opposition in Jerusalem would be more than he could overcome at that moment. Leaving quickly with his friends and faithful bodyguards, the Cherethites and Pelethites (v. 18), the long humiliating journey of the king began. This must have been one of the darkest moments in David's life, for his humiliation did not come at the hands of great Philistine kings or outstanding monarchs from Egypt, but from his own son whom he had restored to royal favor.

At first he considered the presence of the Ark of the Covenant very important and therefore took it with him (vv. 23-24); how-

---

[100]*David.* Quoted in S. Goldman, *op. cit.,* p. 277.

ever, it was later decided that the Ark could not guarantee success, and it was returned to Jerusalem. This act on the part of David indicated that he had now turned the whole situation over to God for final disposition. He was convinced that God would work out His will to perfection. When David heard that Ahithophel, one of his more capable advisors, had joined the rebellion, he employed the services of Hushai, an aged advisor and friend, to infiltrate Absalom's court organization. This was done in order that he might counteract the proposals of Ahithophel.

As David continued his journey from Jerusalem eastward, he was met by the servant of Mephibosheth whose name was Ziba. He brought a few gifts and two asses for David and the royal family, a small price to pay for advancement and recognition by the king. Ziba apparently convinced David that Mephibosheth had cast his lot with Absalom, a story that David should not have accepted immediately since he did not have the opportunity to confirm it, but the tension and pressure of the moment had dulled the keen judicial senses of David so that he believed the story without question and honored the request of the servant. Commentators have agreed that it is rather doubtful that Mephibosheth would have so easily joined the revolt of Absalom. As a cripple he had little to gain by being involved in a revolution of this type. Surely he did not suppose that friendship with Absalom would open up the way for his accession to the throne.

As David continued eastward to Bahurim he was met by Shimei, a member of Saul's household. He evidently stood on the hill that overlooked the road followed by David and his company and cast stones at the king and his servants (16:5-6). He cursed David charging that he was "a bloody man and a man of Belial" (Heb. *'iš haddāmîm we'iš habbelîyā'al*). It could well be that Shimei was accusing David of the murders of Abner (3:27-39), Ish-bosheth (4:1-12), and Uriah (11:15-27). The patience and restraint that David showed on this occasion was most amazing indeed. One should recall the very opposite attitude when encountered by the slanderous words of Nabal (I Sam. 25:2 ff.). On that occasion he was prepared to take the life of that man without hesitation. It will be remembered that through the wisdom of Abigail he was spared the embarrassment of meaningless retaliation. That lesson had been well learned and the patience exhibited on this occasion indicated that David had committed the whole affair into the hands of his God. It is also possible that David regarded the charges of Shimei as justified to the extent that he had committed murder with regard to Uriah. This chapter concludes with Absalom's entry into Jerusalem and the organization of his royal court (vv. 15-23).

That the rebellion of Absalom had been generally sucessful and widespread is indicated by the words of both the elders and the people of Israel recorded in verse 4. They were prepared to destroy the household of David completely and remove any possibility of restoration to the throne. As one remembers the Davidic covenant recorded in II Samuel 7, it becomes apparent that this situation must have been a tension-filled, drama-packed one. Providentially the Lord took control of the situation through the counsel of Hushai who advised Absalom in such a way as to give David time to organize and to prepare for a military encounter with the forces of Absalom. The proposal of Hushai seemed not only workable, but desirable in the eyes of the elders. The two major points of Hushai's counter proposal were that: (1) a larger army was needed than Absalom had at his command at this time. In other words, an encounter with David with such a small army would result in a humiliating defeat for the young king. (2) He played on the arrogance and pride of the king by suggesting that the king himself lead the army into battle. This appeal to his vanity worked, and the result was that David had the additional time needed to organize his own forces in defense of his throne (17:5-23). The humiliation of failure was too much for Ahithophel and he committed suicide (v. 23).

C. *The Death of Absalom* (18:1–19:8)

Absalom was quite sure of a victory. He reorganized the armies under the leadership of Amasa (17:25) and had gathered a considerable number of people together from the various tribes. However, it is clear that Absalom had not calculated the continued popularity of David and the support which he had among many of the tribes. David and his men gathered themselves together at the site known as Mahanaim, probably a fortified city not far from the ford of Jabbok. In preparation for the encounter David divided his men into three companies (v. 2). The three-pronged attack was a common military maneuver of this period (cf. Judg. 7:16; I Sam. 11:11; 13:17). David gave specific instruction that Absalom, his son, should not be harmed if he participated in the battle (v. 5). As it turned out, the newly, and probably poorly, organized armies of Absalom were no match for the seasoned soldiers of David. A slaughter of over 24,000 men was the result of this encounter (v. 7). More tragic for David, however, was the death of Absalom. As Absalom rode upon a mule, his head was caught in the branches of an oak tree and while suspended in this tree Joab had the young man slain (vv. 9-17). Joab, of course, was a ruthless, cold military leader. He did not view Absalom as the son of David, but as an enemy of David and a threat to his throne. With this in mind, he took the life of Absalom in disobedience to David's specific command. It might be pointed out that Absalom's death did not result from excessively long hair which was caught in the tree as it is usually suggested. The text merely indicates that he was suspended from the tree by his head (v. 9). David was quickly informed of the victory and also of the tragic death of his son. The concluding words of Chapter 18 should be a sober reminder to all believers that sin has far reaching and tragic consequences. Surely David did not anticipate uttering the words recorded in verse 33 when he engaged in adulterous acts with Bath-sheba. The pitiful cries of David are a solemn warning that there is a price attached to sin and disobedience.

The sorrow and mourning of David became a matter of concern of Joab. His sad disposition was apparently affecting the morale of David's armies, and a stern rebuke from Joab helped David to get control of himself and look toward the future (19:1-8).

II. RETURN AND RESTORATION (19:9—20:26)

The return of David to Jerusalem and his restoration to the throne was not a simple process. The bitter sentiments of some of the people against David as encouraged by Absalom were slow to die out. It took considerable diplomatic communication to restore David in the eyes of many of his countrymen (19:9-40). In addition to this problem there was the developing political division between Israel in the north and the tribe of Judah to the south. This division had been developing over a long period of time. The viewpoints in this strife came out in the open as David prepared to return to Jerusalem and resume his authority. The two political parties were attempting to gain favor and recognition in the royal court. The return of David to Jerusalem was marked not only by victory and rejoicing, but also by tragedy and revolt. Joab, who did not appreciate competition for his position, took the life of Amasa the military general under Absalom (20:4-12). Joab also pursued a man by the name of Sheba who evidently tried to organize another revolt against the throne. Sheba probably assumed that if Absalom could achieve success, he could use the same forces and the same sentiments to his own end. However, Sheba was captured and slain, thus removing the final threat to the security of the throne (20:13-22).

Sometime in the latter days of David's reign the land was plagued by a famine which lasted for three years (21:1); however, it is evident from verse 7 that the events here narrated must have occurred after David had come to know Mephibosheth. The reason for the famine is given in the latter part of verse 1 of this chapter; namely, because Saul had slain the Gibeonites. This is the only reference to the fact that Saul had committed an offense against the Gibeonites. The details of Saul's action are not given, but his motives are (v. 2). Some feel that this is a reference to the slaying of the priests of Nob (I Sam. 22:18) to whom the Gibeonites were attached as laborers. In slaying the priests, Saul had destroyed their means of support and was, therefore, virtually guilty of slaying them. Others feel that Saul was merely trying to rid the land of the remnant of heathen in order that Israel and Judah might move and grow in more freedom. In any event, it should be observed that covenant-making was no small part of life in the ancient Near East. The covenant made by Joshua some four hundred years before Saul was still valid and had to be respected (cf. Josh. 9:15 ff.).

According to verse 2, the Gibeonites were descendants of the Amorites. This presents a problem because according to Joshua 9:7 and 11:9 the people of Gibeon were Hivites. In many listings of the native inhabitants of Palestine the Hivites are clearly distinguished from the Amorites (see Gen. 10:16-17; Josh. 9:1; 11:3; 12:8). The problem is probably resolved by recognizing that the term "Amorite" is often employed in a comprehensive sense somewhat equivalent to the word "Canaanite" as meaning any of the inhabitants of Canaan (cf. Gen. 15:16; Deut. 1:27). The term "Amorite" sometimes denotes more particularly the inhabitants of the hill country of Palestine as distinct from the Canaanites of the plain (Num. 13:29; Deut. 1:7, 20).

The Gibeonites came to David requiring restitution for the injustice done to them. They would not settle for a mere payment of silver or for the death of any Israelite except the sons of Saul (21:4-6). David probably recognized the legitimacy of their complaint and willingly turned over the sons of Saul to them. The question has been raised as to whether one can reconcile the death of Saul's sons with the command of Moses in Deuteronomy 24:16. Rabbi Jochanan's comment on this problem was, "It is better that a law of the Torah should be overridden than God's name should be publicly profaned (by the failure to expiate Saul's breach of the oath to the Gibeonites)."[101] However, it is more likely that Saul's sons had been directly implicated in the attack on the Gibeonites and therefore received just punishment for their own evil deeds.

III. CONFLICT WITH THE PHILISTINES (21:15-22)

The events described in these verses probably span a period from the revolt of Absalom to the last days of David. It is apparent that the Philistines took the occasion of Absalom's revolt and the subsequent confusion to attack the borders of Israel. The record of these battles is a summary of a number of encounters that took place during this period of time. The battle fought at Gob presents a problem with regard to information concerning the death of Goliath (v. 19). According to this verse, the man who killed Goliath, the Gittite, was Elhanan. It will be noted that the words "the brother of" are not part of the Hebrew text. This expression does occur in the parallel account of I Chronicles

---

[101]*Yebamoth.* Quoted in S. Goldman, *op. cit.,* p. 277.

20:5. To solve the problem of the reading of this verse in Samuel
some have suggested that there were two Goliaths, having the
same name and both descendants of the Gittites.[102] Most commentators, however, feel that the reading of the text in I Chronicles is the correct one and that the text of II Samuel suffers from
a minor scribal omission.[103]

IV. APPENDIX (22:1–24:25)

A. *A Psalm of Praise* (22:1-51)

The psalm before us reflects the thinking of David in his later
years. He was able to look back over the years of blessing and
divine provision, giving him victories over his enemies and establishing his throne. This psalm appears as Psalm 18. Interestingly, verse 1 of this chapter provides the basis for the title of
Psalm 18. This is a psalm of triumph and deliverance. There is
recognition of David's problems and God's deliverance (vv. 2-
21). The psalm also asserts the integrity of David and the just
feelings of God with him throughout his career (vv. 22-46).
While some have attempted to deny Davidic authorship to this
psalm, the majority of commentators recognize the hand of David in its composition. The psalm clearly reflects the attitudes
and the involvements of King David. There is no other individual who could have given such intimate expression to the frustrations and joys of kingship as expressed in this psalm.

B. *David's Last Words* (23:1-7)

The last words of David are not to be regarded as his final
testament which is recorded in I Kings 2:2 ff., but his last formal
utterance and perhaps the last psalm which he composed. It is
interesting that the Hebrew text of verse 1 uses the expression
neʾum dāwid. The Hebrew term *neʾum* is generally employed to
indicate a direct divine utterance or a message given through
the prophets. The word is not usually employed to designate
ordinary human speech, although false prophets many times em-

[102]See S. Goldman, *op. cit.*, p. 324.
[103]C. F. Keil and F. Delitzsch, *op. cit.*, p. 466.

ployed the word in order to give credibility to their message (cf. Jer. 23:31).

The identification of David as "the sweet psalmist of Israel" is interesting and informative. Some scholars have regarded this expression merely as an indication that David was the subject of many of the songs of Israel; however, in the light of the words that precede and follow this expression, it seems clear that authorship is involved. Furthermore, it is made clear in verse 2 that the songs of David were the result of divine inspiration.

C. *A Gallery of Mighty Men* (23:8-39)

The remainder of this chapter is occupied with a list of some of David's outstanding soldiers. This list also appears in I Chronicles 11:11-41 with slight variations. These were men who rendered to David outstanding service and were responsible for his numerous military successes. It is interesting to note that among the great men of David, Uriah the Hittite is listed (v. 39).

D. *The Numbering of the People* (24:1-25)

The first verse of this chapter presents a problem because of the parallel passage in I Chronicles 21:1-6. According to the Samuel passage it was the Lord who moved David to number the people of Israel. This assumes, of course, that the antecedent of the pronoun "he" is the Lord. In the parallel passage of Chronicles, however, it clearly states that Satan was the one who moved David to number the people (I Chron. 21:1). A number of suggested solutions have been given to this problem. One writer argues that it was the "anger of Jehovah" that prompted David to number the people of Israel and Judah.[104] This view takes the subject of the first independent clause and makes it the subject of the second independent clause. While this is remotely possible, it most certainly makes the grammar very awkward and strained. A second view translates the Hebrew word *śāṭān* found in I Chronicles 21:1 as "an adversary" rather than the personal name Satan. It was an adversary of David who prompted

---

[104]Abarbinel, quoted in John Gill, *An Exposition of the Old Testament* (London: Wm. H. Collingridge, 1853), II, p. 311.

him to muster the people together for warfare.[105] Those supporting this theory argue that there is no article prefix to the noun
as in Job 1:6, 7, 8; 2:1, 2. The term, therefore, must have reference to someone other than Satan himself. They also point out
the Hadad and Rezon were "satans" to both Solomon and Israel
(I Kings 11:14-23, 25). It is the latter usage of the term that they
feel the writer of Chronicles was employing. Other commentators have felt that it was Satan himself who initiated David's
numbering of the people, perhaps in disobedience to a command
of God.[106] Those holding this view point out that God could not
be angry with David if He had moved David to commit this act.
The final viewpoint proposed by scholars, and that which appears to be more popular, is that the Chronicles account and the
Samuel account merely reflect two aspects of the same incident.
Satan was the immediate cause of David's action, but, theologically speaking, God was the ultimate cause in that He did not
prevent the incident from occurring. In other words, it was actually Satan who instigated the pride and ambition that led David to increase the size of his army, perhaps unnecessarily.[107]
In the light of all factors involved, it appears that the last view is
preferable.

Another problem associated with this passage is the nature of
David's act. In what did David's sin consist? A number of suggestions have been given. Josephus felt that David forgot the
commands of Moses in that he did not collect a half of a shekel
for the Lord for every head counted.[108] Others have suggested
that it was the attitude of David that brought God's anger and
condemnation. David commanded the census out of an attitude
of pride and vanity, and the purpose of the numbering was to
serve selfish ends only. Others feel that David was over-expand-

[105]Arthur Hervey, "II Samuel," *The Holy Bible with Explanatory and
Critical Commentary*, W. F. C. Cook, ed. (New York: Scribner, Armstrong
& Co., n.d.), II, p. 458.

[106]Joseph Bensen, *Bensen's Commentary* (New York: Carlton and Porter,
n.d.), I, pp. 948-949.

[107]See Francis Nichol, *op. cit.*, p. 710; F. Gardner, *op. cit.*, p. 507 and
C. F. Keil and F. Delitzsch, *op. cit.*, p. 503.

[108]*Ant.* VII.13.1 (cf. Exod. 30:12).

ing his military potential and perhaps placing upon the people excessive burdens.

In any event, it is clear that God was dissatisfied with perhaps the motives, goals and the actions of David, and brought judgment. David, interestingly enough, was given a choice of punishment (v. 13). He selected the three days of pestilence and this resulted in the death of 70,000 men according to verse 15. The repentance of David and his sacrifice to the Lord caused the Lord to cease judgment upon the people and to have mercy upon David (vv. 16-25).

The book of II Samuel, therefore, concludes on a note of sorrow just as it began. David had enjoyed moments of great success and yet, in spite of his wisdom and political genius, as a father he failed within his own household. David's greatest heartaches came not from the enemies on the outside, but from his own family. It was not the weak hands of David that failed him, but a weak heart which allowed him to enter into an adulterous relationship with Bath-sheba. The results of David's reign, however, were not all negative. It is very clear from a military and political point of view that David had fully established the kingdom of Israel. He had given its borders recognition and protection. He had achieved international respect and recognition for Israel in a very brief period of time. This great kingdom soon was to pass into the hands of Solomon, a young man with equal capabilities and gifts.

I KINGS 1-11

Chapter 13

SOLOMON: THE EARLY YEARS
(I Kings 1–5)

The continuation and the conclusion of the story of the united monarchy is found in the first eleven chapters of the book of I Kings. The accounts of the death of David and the rise of Solomon are filled with intrigue and excitement. The early years of Solomon were golden years of prosperity and success. Solomon received a kingdom which was well established and internationally recognized; however, in the process of time, through the economic and physical exploitation of the land, Solomon's power and influence began to decline.

I. INTRODUCTION TO THE BOOKS OF KINGS

A. *The Title*

The Hebrew title to the books is *melākîm* ("kings") and, like the books of Samuel, were originally one book. The books of Kings get their title from the type of leadership characteristic of that period. The Septuagint calls these books the Third and Fourth Books of the Kingdom. The First and Second Books of the Kingdom were the books of Samuel. Kings continued as an undivided book in the Hebrew text until the time of Daniel Bomberg (1516-1517). I Kings begins with the death of David and the accession of Solomon and concludes with the reign of Jehoram in Judah and Ahaziah in Israel. II Kings continues the account of Ahaziah's reign and concludes with the destruction of the kingdom of Judah.

B. *Author*

Ancient Jewish tradition found in the Talmud asserts that Jeremiah was the author of the books of Kings. This theory has some credibility, for there are striking similarities between parts of the Kings and material found in the book of Jeremiah (cf. II Kings 24:18–25:30 with Jer. 52). Also in favor of this theory is the fact that there is no mention of Jeremiah himself in chapters which deal with Josiah and his successors. It is quite clear, however, that the major portion of material in the books of Kings represents a composite authorship. The final chapters of the books must have been written by someone other than Jeremiah, for Jeremiah was in Egypt at that time (cf. Jer. 43:1-8), and the description is that of one living in Babylon. The historian makes it plain that he had at least three sources for this history (I Kings 11:41; 14:19, 29). A number of individuals were associated with first-hand reports on specific material.[109]

Whoever the writer, it is quite clear that he wrote by divine inspiration and had uttered prophetic truth. No court historian normally would have included the failures and humiliations of King Solomon in the record. The balance, character and the theological content of the material indicate that the Holy Spirit guided in the ultimate production of the record.

C. *The Purpose*

The fundamental purpose of the books of Kings is to continue the history of the theocracy until its conclusion in the Babylonian exile. Even though the author's chief concern was with the Davidic line, he included considerable material which dealt with the fortunes and failures of the Northern Kingdom. The writer's approach to the subject matter was from the standpoint of the plans and purposes of God as it related to His chosen people. The writings are intensely theological and yet extremely practical. The books of Kings are very important to the Bible student because they give him the cultural and historical background of the ministry of Israel's great prophets.

D. *Basic Outline of I Kings*

1. *The Reign of Solomon* (1:1–11:43)
    a. Solomon's Accession to the Throne (1:1–2:11)
    b. Solomon's Establishment of the Kingdom (2:12–5:18)

---

[109]Nathan, Ahijah, and Iddo (II Chron. 9:29), Shemaiah and Iddo (II Chron. 12:15), Iddo (II Chron. 13:22), Isaiah (II Chron. 26:22; 32:32) and Jehu (I Kings 16:1).

II. SOLOMON'S ACCESSION TO THE THRONE (1:1–2:11)

A. *David's Illness* (1:1-4)

The chapter before us describes the last court intrigue of David's life. At this point he was extremely old and quite ill. According to II Samuel 5:4 he had reached the age of seventy years. As far as can be determined, he was the oldest of the Hebrew kings on record. King David was so weak at this time that he had to be put under the constant care of a young maid by the name of Abishag, a Shunammite (v. 3). It was probably clear to both David and his servants that his days were few in number.

B. *Adonijah's Attempt to Usurp the Throne* (1:5-53)

When Adonijah received word of the serious illness of his father, he immediately took steps to achieve recognition as Israel's next king. Verse 6 gives three reasons why he made his move toward the throne. First, his father had not "displeased him at any time in saying, Why hast thou done so?" Apparently David had never disciplined Adonijah and had never questioned his activities. Thus, he had a free hand in gathering about him court officials and court personnel in Jerusalem. Secondly, he was an attractive man, and such attractiveness would make him a desirable candidate for the throne. Thirdly, he was the oldest living son now that Absalom was dead. David's first-born son, Amnon, was killed by Absalom (II Sam. 13:28 ff.). Chileab (or Daniel, I Chron. 3:1) probably died at a rather young age since nothing is recorded of him. David's third son, Absalom, was slain by Joab's men in battle (II Sam. 18:15).

Adonijah must have commanded the interest of many important individuals. For example, he was able to gain the support of Joab, the captain of the host (v. 7). In addition to that, Abiathar the priest also supported him. Abiathar, it will be remembered, was the great-grandson of Eli (I Sam. 14:3; 22:20), who was descended from Ithamar, the son of Aaron (I Chron. 24:3). A number of court officials, however, refused to join in the proposed move of Adonijah. Those who remained faithful included Zadok the priest, Benaiah, Nathan the prophet, Shimei, and Rei (v. 8). This did not discourage Adonijah, and he proceeded to conduct a public sacrifice in En-rogel (v. 9).

When Nathan the prophet received word of the intentions of Adonijah, he immediately made an appeal to Bath-sheba to intercede on the behalf of Solomon. Apparently David had, at an earlier time, solemnly promised to Bath-sheba and perhaps to Nathan that Solomon would be the next king. This promise on the part of David might have been made at the time of Solomon's birth, or perhaps on the occasion of Absalom's rebellion and death. In any event, Bath-sheba proceeded to inform David of the intentions of Adonijah and pleaded on Solomon's behalf. David recognized the danger at hand and called for Zadok the priest in order that Solomon might be properly anointed and declared Israel's next king (vv. 32-39). Zadok took the oil from the tabernacle and anointed Solomon (v. 39). This was then followed with the public proclamation of the Solomonic anointing and his accession to the throne (v. 4).

While this was going on, Adonijah had organized a banquet which included prominent people from Jerusalem, including Joab and those who supported his claims to the throne. His "ten shekel a plate fund raising dinner" was going along quite smoothly until the shouts of recognition for Solomon were heard outside the building. It was not long before the guests realized that they had committed themselves to a losing cause, and little by little they left the banquet (v. 49). It did not take Adonijah very long to realize that his attempts to take the throne were abortive and his life was now in danger. In order to secure mercy he fled to the tabernacle and there caught hold on the horns of the altar (v. 50). Solomon, evidently, did not consider Adonijah a serious threat any longer and granted him mercy as long as he relinquished any further claims to the throne.

C. *David's Charge to Solomon* (2:1-11)

David's final admonitions to his son Solomon were, first of all, spiritually and theologically oriented (vv. 1-4). David made it clear that obedience to the Word of God was the key to prosperity (v. 3; cf. Josh. 1:8; Ps. 1:2). Following this admonition, he cited certain individuals who should be removed from the royal court in order that further trouble should not develop. Among those to be removed was Joab who had murdered Absalom (II Sam. 18:14 ff.) and Amasa (II Sam. 19:13; 20:8-10). Joab had also supported Adonijah in his attempt to seize the throne (I Kings 1:7). The second individual cited by David for punishment was Shimei (v. 8). David remembered the curses and the stones thrown by Shimei when he had to flee during the rebellion of Absalom (II Sam. 16:5-13). Even though Shimei sought pardon after the rebellion, it was possible that he might turn against the throne again. David's instructions in this area were not all negative, however. He remembered the kindness of Barzillai, the man who helped sustain him in those days of confusion and humiliation when he had to flee Jerusalem as a result of Absalom's revolt (II Sam. 19:31 ff.). Barzillai was to be given preferential treatment as a reward for his faithfulness to the throne.

After a very eventful reign of approximately forty years (v. 11), David died and was buried in Jerusalem (v. 10; cf. Neh. 3:15-16).

III. THE KINGDOM ESTABLISHED AND ENRICHED (2:12—5:18)

A. *The Removal of David's Adversaries* (2:12-46)

The first individual to fall under the punitive wrath of Solomon was Adonijah, who had not ceased in his attempt to secure royal recognition. This time Adonijah came to Bath-sheba, Solomon's mother, and requested that Abishag, one of David's concubines, be given to him as a wife (vv. 13-17). Bath-sheba, not fully understanding all the intentions of Adonijah, went to Solomon and presented Adonijah's request. Solomon immediately recognized the intentions of Adonijah. The harem of a king was the sole property of his successor and a sign of royalty. Having already failed in his first attempt to take the throne, Adonijah was attempting by a more subtle means to gain his objectives. Solomon immediately recognized the plan and condemned him to death (vv. 22-25).

Following this, Abiathar the priest was removed from office and Zadok became the sole priest at this time (vv. 26, 27, 35). Joab heard of the executions and the moves of Solomon and decided to plead for mercy. He did this in the same manner as Adonijah had done at an earlier time (cf. v. 28 with 1:50). To take hold on the horns of the altar was to claim the right of sanctuary, but it should be noted that this right was denied to a wilful murderer (cf. Exod. 21:14). Because of Joab's murders and his participation in the revolt led by Adonijah, he, like Adonijah, was slain (vv. 31-35). The last individual to fall under the wrath of Solomon was Shimei. His death did not come merely as a result of his cursing David, but because of his refusal to follow special restrictions placed upon him by King Solomon (vv. 36-45). The removal of these individuals cleared the way for a complete rebuilding of the royal court and a guarantee of its firm establishment.

B. *Political Alliance with Egypt* (3:1-3)

It is interesting to compare the political and military strategies of Israel's first kings. King Saul, on the one hand, was occupied with defensive military measures for the most part. His reign was characterized by reactions to Philistine raids and military pressure put on Israel from other areas. David, on the other hand, not only defended the territory which Israel held, but also expanded her borders and secured those borders with the use of a series of fortresses. David also initiated and expanded Israel's commercial resources. Agreements with the Phoenicians regarding trade had been reached. David also used the process of royal marriage for the purpose of securing royal alliances and concluding treaties. Such a practice was common in the ancient Near East. It will be remembered that in the very early days of David's reign he employed this approach by marrying the daughter of Talmai, king of Geshur (II Sam. 3:3; I Chron. 3:2).

Solomon, however, brought to Israel its most complete and intricate organization. He initiated major changes in Israel's military system by introducing chariotry as an essential fighting force. As will be noted later, he organized the Northern Kingdom into twelve administrative districts to provide food for the royal court. Solomon expanded previous commercial contacts and created new commercial monopolies. He also embarked upon a very energetic building program which was carried out in various parts of the land.

The marriage of Solomon to Pharaoh's daughter is something of great significance (3:1). "As far as we know, there is no real example of Pharaoh's daughter given in marriage to a foreign royal house, although the pharaohs quite frequently married daughters of foreign rulers."[110] We know for example that Kadash-manharbe, king of Babylon, did ask for the hand of Akhenaton's daughter and was flatly refused in rather strong language. In Amarna Letter IV, the following words appear as an answer from King Akhenaton: ". . . from of old, a daughter of the king of Egypt has not been given to anyone."[111] The marriage of Solomon to Pharaoh's daughter, therefore, has important political and military implications. It indicates, on the one hand, that Egypt, under the leadership of the Twenty-first Dynasty, was extremely weak. On the other hand, it indicates the military and political superiority of the Solomonic empire over Egypt. The precise identity of Solomon's father-in-law in Egypt is not completely clear at this point. The most widely accepted candidate is Psusennes II who was the last king of the Twenty-first Dynasty. Malamat, however, suggests the possibility of Simanon, the pred-

---

[110]A. Malamat, "The Kingdom of David and Solomon in its Contact with Egypt and Aram Naharaim," *The Biblical Archaeologist*, XXI, (Dec., 1958), p. 97.

[111]Amarna Tablet EA, 4, II, 6-7 quoted in A. Malamat, *Ibid.*, p. 98. Cf. also A. Malamat, "Aspects of the Foreign Policies of David and Solomon," *Journal of Near Eastern Studies*, XXII, 1 (Jan., 1963), p. 10.

ecessor of Psusennes.[112] Further proof of Solomonic prestige is
seen in the dowry given to Solomon on the occasion of his marriage. The city of Gezer, which had been taken by the Egyptians, was used as a wedding gift (I Kings 9:16).

C. *A Prayer for Wisdom* (3:5-28)

While at Gibeon worshipping (v. 4), Solomon received a
dream in which the Lord asked him what he would desire (v.
5). In all probability this dream represented God's answer to a
previous request on the part of Solomon. The use of dreams as a
means of divine revelation was not uncommon either in this period or in later periods. Solomon's response included a recognition of God's faithfulness to the throne (v. 6), and perhaps most
significant, a recognition of his inexperience (v. 7). The expression "I am but a little child" does not mean that Solomon
was a young boy when he took the throne. Josephus, for example, asserted that Solomon was only fourteen years old at this
time.[113] This idea is not correct, for "little child" is merely an
assertion of humility and a recognition that from the standpoint
of experience, he was like a child. His principal request, as he
viewed the greatness of his task (v. 8), was that he might be
given "an understanding heart to judge thy people" (v. 9). It is
instructive, indeed, that Solomon brought to the throne a very
high view of the people of God. He looked up to his task, not
down to it. The attitude and request of Solomon pleased the
Lord and his prayer was answered (vv. 10-15). The proof of
God's blessing in Solomon's life and the fact that he had been
given the gift of practical wisdom is seen in the concluding
verses of this chapter which describe one of his first judicial
cases (vv. 16-28).

D. *Organization of the Kingdom* (4:1–5:18)

1. *The King's Officials* (4:1-20)

The court organization adopted by Solomon was principally
that established by David. The significant difference between

---

[112]"The Kingdom of David and Solomon in its Contact with Egypt and
Aram Naharaim," *op. cit.*, p. 99.
    [113]*Ant.*, VIII.7.8.

David's list of officers (II Sam. 8:16-18; 20:23-26) and Solomon's is that the first officer in David's was the captain of the host; whereas, the first officer listed in Solomon's court was the priest (v. 2). Basically, Solomon's organization of the royal court represented an expansion of the system established by David. One of the offices was the "recorder" (v. 3) which Jehoshaphat held during David's reign (I Chron. 18:15) and apparently continued to hold into the reign of Solomon. This office was, in effect, that of a court annalist whose duty it was to record events as they occurred and who probably was responsible for the official archives of the realm (cf. II Kings 18:18-37; II Chron. 34:8). The "captain of the hosts" was Benaiah (v. 4), with Zadok and Abiathar as the chief priests. Adoniram was set over the "tribute" (v. 6), which is better translated "forced labor" or "levy." This office was evidently established in the latter part of David's reign (II Sam. 20:24), for his earlier list of offices does not include the one here mentioned (cf. II Sam. 8:16-18).

Solomon organized the Northern Kingdom and Transjordan into twelve districts headed up by one governor in each district. The twelve districts had no consistent relationship to the original division of land among the twelve tribes, but were related primarily to the twelve months of the year.[114] Each governor was responsible for supplying the needs of the royal court for one month (v. 7). In order to guarantee the fidelity of several of the governors, his daughters were given to them as wives (cf. vv. 11, 15).

2. The Wealth of the Kingdom (4:21-28)

Solomon's prestige and power reached all the way from the river Euphrates in the north to the border of Egypt (v. 21). The amount of food required for one day in the royal court was so significant that it was included in the official record found in this chapter (vv. 22-23). Solomon's success was also witnessed in his ability to guarantee property rights and secure peace for the land (v. 25). His military strength and the expansion of the char-

---

[114]See Yohanan Aharoni and Michael Avi-Yonah, *The Macmillan Bible Atlas* (New York: The Macmillan Co., 1968), p. 72.

iot forces were a particular characteristic of Solomonic organization. Verse 26 indicates that Solomon possessed "forty thousand
stalls of horses for his chariots." The parallel passage in II Chronicles 9:25 reads "four thousand." Quite evidently the Kings passage reflects a copyist's error and the better reading is "four thousand."

3. *The Fame of the King* (4:29-34)

While only a few proverbs of Solomon have actually been preserved, it seems clear from verse 32 that he was known for many
proverbs and songs. The fact that he had a keen interest and
understanding of natural phenomena, as noted in verse 33, might
be a clue to the authorship of both Ecclesiastes and the Song of
Solomon.

4. *Building Preparations* (5:1-18)

As Solomon began to make preparations for the building of
the temple, he was contacted by Hiram, king of Tyre, who had
had earlier trade agreements with David (v. 1; cf. II Sam. 5:11).
Since the land was now enjoying relative peace (vv. 3-4), it was
possible for Solomon to initiate and complete the building of
the temple. A formal written agreement was drawn up between
Solomon and Hiram including not only the exchange of materials,
but also laborers (cf. vv. 6-12 and II Chron. 2:11). Josephus
stated that copies of the letters between Hiram and Solomon
were still in existence in the days of Menandar (*c.* 300 B.C.)
and could be seen in the archives of Tyre.[115] In order to guarantee success for the project, Solomon "raised a levy out of all Israel" (v. 13) and as far as can be determined this was the first
major levy ever raised from the tribes. During the reign of David, strangers were used in this manner (I Chron. 22:2), and apparently Israelites were used only in a limited way. It will be
remembered that Samuel warned Israel that such a policy would
result from monarchial leadership as Israel desired it (I Sam. 8:
16). The requirement for those taken in levy was that they were
to work one month out of three (v. 14). This was done in order

---

[115]*Ant.* VIII.5.3.

that there would not be widespread discontent. Much of the skilled work, however, was done by Hiram's men who were known for their outstanding ability (vv. 6, 18). The use of the word "stonesquarers" (v. 18) is probably not the best translation of the Hebrew. The correct reading of the Hebrew text is "Giblites." These were the inhabitants of Gebal or Byblos (cf. Ezek. 27:9), an important coastal city of Phoenicia.

While Solomon achieved a high degree of organization and effective production, it led to rapid and widespread bureaucratization in his kingdom. This, in turn, led to the rapid decline of tribal rights and reduction of the force of covenant law. That Solomon's policies ultimately led to widespread discontent is made clear when Rehoboam took the throne after Solomon's death (cf. I Kings 12:3-4). While the days of Solomon were indeed the golden days of monarchial success, they were also days of personal and tribal humiliation. Solomon's success came at the high price of individual freedom and tribal sovereignty.

Chapter 14

SOLOMON: THE GREAT YEARS
(I Kings 6–11)

The wealth and splendor of the Solomonic kingdom was unparalleled in Hebrew history. Solomon was successful not only in territorial expansion and the establishment of foreign alliances, but brought to Israel sophistication in government operations. The chapters before us give significant insight into the wealth and power of the kingdom of Israel during Solomon's reign. His great achievements included construction of the temple and a magnificent palace in Jerusalem, as well as other structures of note throughout the land. His commercial and domestic policies produced tremendous wealth and prestige within the kingdom. Solomon achieved a degree of international recognition which was never matched in the remaining years of Israel's history.

I. THE TEMPLE (6:1-38; 8:1; 9:9)

A. *The Date of Construction* (6:1)

The chronological information supplied in this verse is of great importance to Bible students. If it is numerically correct, the date of the exodus must be placed in the middle of the fifteenth century B.C. According to the information supplied, the fourth year of Solomon represented a point in time which was 480 years after the exodus from Egypt. The fourth year of Solomon is generally regarded as being 967/966 B.C. This being the case, the exodus would have taken place approximately 1445 B.C. This date, however, conflicts with what some scholars feel to be stronger evidence in favor of a thirteenth century B.C. date for the exodus. In the light of what they feel to be more compelling evidence, this verse is considered symbolic and the "four hundred eighty" merely represents twelve generations of forty years each and, according to this view, is not intended to be taken literally. However, this interpretation has serious weaknesses. In the first place, the text is in no way poetic or symbolical. It appears in a serious narrative portion and is a very important state-

180

Air View of Jerusalem showing the Temple area and Old City. Matson Photo Service

ment in the light of the subject matter discussed. Second, it is in agreement with other Biblical data regarding the time lapse between the exodus and the rise of the monarchy.[116] Third, while the Septuagint gives the figure 440 years instead of 480, the Hebrew text does not have any significant variants.[117] In the light of these considerations, therefore, it seems advisable to accept the numerical data as being accurate and dependable.

B. *Its Size and Appearance* (6:2 ff.)

According to verse 2, the temple proper was 60 cubits long and 20 cubits wide, exactly twice the size of the Tabernacle (cf. Exod. 26:16, 18). If the cubit is regarded as eighteen inches, then the floor plan of the temple would have been 90 x 30 feet. The temple proper was divided into two sections. The inner room or the most Holy Place was a cube measuring 20 x 20 x 20 cubits (6:16, 20). The other room or the outer chamber called the Holy Place measured 40 x 20 cubits.

The finishing work and decoration of the temple proper was nothing short of spectacular. The floor and walls were made of stone covered with cedar and then overlaid with gold (I Kings 6:16, 21, 22). Around the temple proper, on the two sides and back, special chambers were added (6:5-6). In front of the temple there was a porch which measured 20 cubits long and 10 cubits wide (6:3). Two large pillars stood in front of the temple which were given the names Jachin and Boaz (7:21).

Even though nothing remains of Solomon's temple in Jerusalem, one is able to reconstruct major portions of the temple on the basis of archaeological data. Excavations of the Oriental Institute of the University of Chicago at Tell Tainat (ancient Hattina) in Syria have recovered a small chapel dating to the eighth century B.C. This temple has some very similar features to that of the temple of Solomon.[118] Of even greater interest, however, is the

---

[116]See John J. Davis, *Conquest and Crisis,* pp. 17-18.
[117]Josephus gives the figure variously as 592 or 612 (*Ant.,* VIII.3.1 and XX.10.1).
[118]See G. E. Wright, *Biblical Archaeology* (Philadelphia: The Westminster Press, 1957), p. 136 ff.

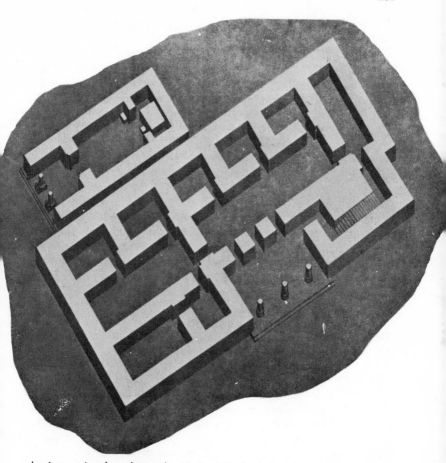

An isometric plan drawn by H. D. Hill depicting the residence (fore-ground) and chapel (background) of the eighth century B.C. rulers at Tell Tainat. Courtesy of the Oriental Institute, University of Chicago

discovery of an Israelite (Kenite?) temple dating to the tenth century B.C. at Tell Arad.

Together with its side rooms, it was a building over sixty-five foot long, and forty-nine foot broad, occupying a vital part of the relatively small citadel. The entrance was on the eastern

side, with the holy of holies toward the west. Its original plan
was simple and symmetric . . .[119]

The temple of Solomon was constructed with Phoenician skilled
labor and included a number of Phoenician influences; however,
the temple should not be regarded as solely Phoenician in its design. Its plan was probably based on the general layout of the
Tabernacle and its layout follows traditions associated with that
structure rather than contemporary cult centers.

In the Holy of Holies the old Mosaic ark of the covenant was
placed with its two golden cherubims above the mercy seat. The
ark had an added feature in Solomon's temple in that it was
placed between two additional figures of cherubim made of olive
wood and overlaid with gold (cf. 6:23, 28; II Chron. 3:10-13).
Inside the Holy Place was the altar of incense covered with cedar and overlaid with gold (6:20, 22; 7:48). Instead of the single
golden candlestick as in the Tabernacle, there were now ten. Five
were placed on one side and five on the other side of the Holy
Place. Instead of only one table of shewbread, there were now
ten, five on each side of the room with all utensils made of gold.
The inner court had the familiar brazen altar of burnt offering
and the "bronze sea" which, in effect, took the place of the "la-
ver" of the Tabernacle. It was given the name "moulten sea" because of its great size.[120]

In addition to the seven years used to complete the temple
(6:37-38), Solomon spent thirteen years constructing his own palace (7:1). The "house of the forest of Lebanon" mentioned in
verse 2 has been regarded by some as to have been a structure
built in the mountains of Lebanon. Others suppose that Solomon's house (v. 1), the house of the forest of Lebanon (v. 2),
and the house of Pharaoh's daughter (v. 8) were three distinct
and separate buildings in Jerusalem. Yet another view on these

---

[119]Yohanan Aharoni, "Arad: Its Inscriptions and Temple," *The Biblical
Archaeologist*, XXXI, 1 (Feb., 1968), p. 19.

[120]For further details on the temple and its furnishings see "Temple,"
The International Standard Bible Encyclopedia, V, pp. 2930-2936, and
G. Ernest Wright, "The Steven's Reconstruction of the Solomonic Temple,"
The Biblical Archaeologist, XVIII, 2 (May, 1955).
Merrill F. Unger, *Archaeology and the Old Testament*, pp. 228-234. Also,

expressions is that they merely reflect three sections of the one main palace known as the "king's house" (9:10). One thing is clear, however, and that is that Solomon embarked upon a massive building program not only in Jerusalem, but in other parts of the country as well. In I Kings 9:15 we are informed that his building projects included Millo, the wall of Jerusalem, Hazor, Megiddo and Gezer. A great deal of archaeological light has been shed on the work at Megiddo and particularly at Hazor.[121]

II. SOLOMON'S COMMERCIAL ENTERPRISES

A. *The Navy*

According to I Kings 9:26-28 and 10:22 (II Chron. 8:17-18), Solomon had an extensive fleet of ships located at Ezion-geber which is located on the Gulf of Aqaba. In all probability the port was under the supervision of Phoenicians who were known for their ship building capabilities (cf. 10:22). Archaeological work conducted at Tell el-Kheleifeh or Biblical Ezion-geber indicates that it was not only extensively occupied in the days of Solomon, but was used as a smelting operation. Among other structures found at this site was a well-built structure with high floors designed and used either as a storehouse or granary.[122] Regarding the smelting activities carried on at Ezion-geber, Nelson Glueck says the following:

> . . . We should like to underscore the fact that industrial and metallurgical activities did indeed take place in the various periods of occupation of Tell el-Kheleifeh. Copper slag was definitely found in the excavations as well as remnants of copper implements and vessels. There was, however, little slag compared to the great masses of slag marking numerous Iron I and early Iron II copper mining and smelting sites in the Wadi Arabah where mining and smelting activities also were carried on in Middle Bronze I and late Chalcolithic times.

---

[121]See articles in the *Biblical Archaeologist* by Yigael Yadin: XIX, 1 (Feb., 1956); XX, 2 (May, 1957); XXXII, 3 (Sept., 1969). D. Ussishkin, "King Solomon's Palace and Building 1723 in Megiddo," *Israel Exploration Journal*, XVI, 3 (1966), pp. 174-186.

[122]Nelson Glueck, "Ezion-geber," *The Biblical Archaeologist*, XXVIII, 3 (Sept., 1965), p. 75.

A reconstruction drawing of the NE gate at Megiddo (Stratum IV).
Courtesy of the Oriental Institute, University of Chicago

A Pink-buff Clay Liver Model discovered at Megiddo (Stratum VII).
Courtesy of the Oriental Institute, University of Chicago

A Reconstruction of Building 338 at Megiddo as seen from the NE according to a drawing by L. C. Woolman. Courtesy of the Oriental Institute, University of Chicago

Limestone Altars, Offering Stands and Other Objects found at Mediggo dating to the eleventh century B.C. Courtesy of the Oriental Institute, University of Chicago

The small amount of slag at Tell el-Kheleifeh may be explained by the difference in metallurgical operations as carried out in Wadi Arabah and at Tell el-Kheleifeh. At the latter place, they were devoted, we believe, to remelting the globules of copper ore obtained through several metallurgical processes in the Wadi Arabah smelting sites, in order to shape them in more easily salable ingots or to pour the molten metal into molds for manufacturing purposes. This process would have produced no slag.[123]

New light has also been shed on the nature of Solomon's "navy" or "fleet of Tarshish." Recent studies have indicated that the navy of Solomon was, in effect, a specialized "smeltery" or "refinery fleet" which was responsible for bringing smelted metal home from the colonial mines. The Phoenicians were also probably very much engaged in this activity.[124] In addition to carrying slag and metal materials, Solomon's ships also went to Ophir. This was carried out in collaboration with Hiram, king of Tyre (10:22). The term Ophir probably includes most of the region of South Arabia and was commonly associated with the production of fine gold in the Old Testament (cf. I Kings 10:11; Job 22: 24; Ps. 45:9; Isa. 13:12). Solomon was able to strengthen his ties with the Arabian merchants by virtue of the visit of the queen of Sheba (10:1-13). Many of the objects brought to Israel by Solomon's merchant fleet came from such distant places as Africa, Arabia and parts of the Mediterranean world.

One of Solomon's very important enterprises was the trading of horses and chariots (10:28-29). Many of the purchases made were probably for his own armies, but it is also possible that he provided horses and chariots for other countries as well, perhaps acting as a middleman in the commercial negotiations (cf. 10:26 with 4:26).

In spite of the commercial success of Solomon in these various areas, it is rather clear that near the end of his reign he ran into financial difficulty. After the construction of the elaborate temple and palaces in Jerusalem, he was required to pay Hiram, king

[123]*Ibid.*

[124]See W. F. Albright, *Old Testament Commentary*, p. 51 and his "New Light on the Early History of Phoenician Colonization," *Bulletin of the American Schools of Oriental Research*, LXXXIII, 83 (Oct., 1941), p. 21.

of Tyre, for the wood and labor used. Unlike earlier agreements, he was not able to give Hiram food products from Israel. Instead he gave him twenty cities located in the land of Galilee (9:10-13). This exchange was not satisfactory with Hiram. In all probability the cities were unimportant and nonproductive.

III. APOSTASY AND ITS CONSEQUENCES (11:1-43)

The latter years of Solomon's reign were marked by gradual apostasy and departure from the law. The many marriages which he concluded for purposes of alliance began to influence his spiritual life. In addition to the daughter of Pharaoh, verse 7 indicates that he had 700 wives and princesses as well as 300 concubines. In order to make royal marriages effective it was evidently necessary to build temples for the more important wives living with him in Jerusalem (vv. 5-8). International marriages commonly required the recognition of foreign deities and the intermarriages of Solomon with important princesses of other lands was no exception. As a result of this, the Scripture states that his wives "turned away his heart after other gods" (v. 4). This practice on the part of Solomon diminished the effectiveness of the true temple and made it difficult for the people to distinguish between the true and the false. Foreign deities were given official recognition and this certainly made it difficult to maintain true worship in Israel. As a result of Solomon's disobedience and deep involvement in apostasy, God raised up a number of adversaries to frustrate and humiliate the very proud king. Among these were Hadad the Edomite (v. 14) and, to the north, Rezon a renegade from the Aramaean kings. Within Israel itself a revolt was led by Jeroboam because of the heavy levies placed upon the people of Israel (v. 27). The result of all of this was the clear prophecy that following Solomon's death the kingdom would be divided. Jeroboam was to receive ten tribes to the north (v. 31) and was to uphold God's promise to David, while the house of David would maintain control in the south (v. 32). The turmoil of the final years of Solomon's reign and the division of the kingdom was the direct result of his involvement in idolatry (vv. 33-40). Following the death of Solomon, his son Rehoboam took the throne (v. 43).

This brief look at Solomon has been sufficient to demonstrate his greatness as a king and leader. He was uniquely blessed by God with wisdom above all his contemporaries. The mere possession of wisdom, however, did not guarantee spiritual success. The materialistic interests of Solomon ultimately led him to open idolatry in violation of the law. His life, therefore, is a solemn reminder that wisdom and intellectual genius are only really worthwhile when they are made subject to God's Word.

BIBLIOGRAPHY

Adam, J. McKee. *Biblical Backgrounds*. Nashville: Broadman Press, 1934.

Aharoni, Yohanan. *The Land of the Bible*. Trans. A. F. Rainey. Philadelphia: The Westminster Press, 1962.

Aharoni, Yohanan and Avi-Yonah, Michael. *The Macmillan Bible Atlas*. *New York*: The Macmillan Co., 1968.

Albright, W. F. *Archaeology and the Religion of Israel*. Baltimore: The Johns Hopkins Press, 1953.

————. *The Archaeology of Palestine*. Baltimore: Penguin Books, 1961.

————. *The Biblical Period from Abraham to Ezra*. New York: Harper & Row Publishers, 1949.

————. *From the Stone Age to Christianity*. Baltimore: The Johns Hopkins Press, 1957.

Alleman, H. C. and Flack, E. E. *Old Testament Commentary*. Philadelphia, 1954.

Anderson, Bernhard W. *Understanding the Old Testament*. Englewood Cliffs: Prentice-Hall, Inc., 1957.

Archer, Gleason L. *A Survey of Old Testament Introduction*. Chicago: Moody Press, 1964.

Baly, Denis. *The Geography of the Bible*. New York: Harper & Bros., 1957.

Baxter, J. Sidlow. "Judges to Esther," *Explore the Book*, II. Grand Rapids: Zondervan Publishing House, 1960.

Bensen, Joseph. *Bensen's Commentary*. New York: Carlton and Porter, n.d.

Bright, John. *A History of Israel*. Philadelphia: Westminster Press, 1959.

Brown, Francis, Driver, S. R. and Briggs, Charles. *A Hebrew and English Lexicon of the Old Testament*. Oxford: The Clarendon Press, Corrected Impression, 1952.

Buck, Harry M. *People of the Lord*. New York: The Macmillan Company, 1966.

Burrows, Millar. *What Mean These Stones?* New York: Meridian Books, 1957.

Clarke, Adam. *Clarke's Commentary*. New York: Carlton and Phillips, 1854.

Cook, W. F. C. (ed.) *The Holy Bible with Explanatory and Critical Commentary*. New York: Scribner, Armstrong & Co., n.d.

Davidson, A. B. *The Theology of the Old Testament*. New York: Charles Scribner's Sons, 1907.

Davidson, F., Stibbs, A. M. and Kevan, E. F. (eds.) *New Bible Commentary*. Grand Rapids: Wm. B. Eerdmans Publishing Co., 1953.

Davis, John D. *A Dictionary of the Bible*. Grand Rapids: Baker Book House, 1954.

Davis, John J. *Conquest and Crisis*. Grand Rapids: Baker Book House, 1969.

————. *Biblical Numerology*. Grand Rapids: Baker Book House, 1968.

Douglas, J. D. (ed.) *The New Bible Dictionary*. Grand Rapids: Wm. B. Eerdmans Publishing Co., 1962.

Driver, G. R. *Canaanite Myths and Legends*. Edinburgh: T & T Clark, 1956.

Driver, S. R. *Notes on the Hebrew Text of the Books of Samuel*. Oxford: The Clarendon Press, 1913.

Eissfeldt, O. *The Hebrew Kingdom*. Cambridge: University Press, 1965.

Ellicott, Charles (ed.) *Ellicott's Commentary on the Whole Bible*. Grand Rapids: Zondervan Publishing House, n.d.

Freeman, Hobart E. *An Introduction to the Old Testament Prophets*. Chicago: Moody Press, 1968.

Finegan, Jack. *Handbook of Biblical Chronology*. Princeton: Princeton University Press, 1964.

————. *Light from the Ancient Past*. Princeton: Princeton University Press, 1959.

Gill, John. *An Exposition of the Old Testament*, II. London: Wm. H. Collingridge, 1853.

Goldman, S. "Samuel," *Soncino Books of the Bible*. London: Soncino Press, 1951.

Gordon, Cyrus. *Ugaritic Literature*. Rome: Pontifical Bible Institute, 1949.

————. *The World of the Old Testament*. London: Phoenix House, 1960.

Harrison, R. K. *Introduction to the Old Testament*. Grand Rapids: Wm. B. Eerdmans Publishing Co., 1969.

Heinisch, Paul. *Theology of the Old Testament*. The Liturgical Press, 1955.

Jamieson, R., Fausset, A. R. and Brown, D. (eds.) *Commentary on the Whole Bible*. Grand Rapids: Wm. B. Eerdmans Publishing Co., 1948.

Keil, C. F. and Delitzsch, F. *Biblical Commentary on the Books of Samuel*. Trans. James Martin. Grand Rapids: Wm. B. Eerdmans Publishing Co., 1950.

Kenyon, Kathleen. *Archaeology in the Holy Land*. New York: Frederick A. Praeger, 1960.

Kitchen, K. A. *Ancient Orient and the Old Testament*. Chicago: Inter-Varsity Press, 1966.

Nichol, Francis D. (ed.) *The Seventh-day Adventist Bible Commentary*, II. Review and Herald Publishing Assoc., 1954.

Noth, Martin. *The History of Israel*. New York: Harper & Rowe, 1960.

Oehler, Gustave F. *Theology of the Old Testament*. Grand Rapids: Zondervan Publishing House, n.d.

Orr, James (ed.) *The International Bible Encyclopedia*. Grand Rapids: Wm. B. Eerdmans Publishing Co., 1960.

Payne, J. Barton. *The Theology of the Older Testament*. Grand Rapids: Zondervan Publishing House, 1962.

Pfeiffer, Charles and Harrison, Everett, F., (eds.) *The Wycliffe Bible Commentary*. Chicago: Moody Press, 1962.

Pritchard, James B. *Gibeon, Where the Sun Stood Still*. Princeton, N.J.: Princeton University Press, 1962.

———. (ed.) *Ancient Near Eastern Texts*. New Jersey: Princeton University Press, 1955.

Rowley, H. H. *The Rediscovery of the Old Testament*. Philadelphia: The Westminster Press, 1946.

———. *The Servants of the Lord*. Oxford: Basil Blackwell, 2nd Edition Revised, 1965.

Terry, Milton S. *Biblical Hermeneutics*. Grand Rapids: Zondervan Publishing House, n.d.

Thiele, Edwin J. *The Mysterious Numbers of the Hebrew Kings*. Grand Rapids: Wm. B. Eerdmans Publishing Co., Rev. ed., 1965.

Thomas, D. Winton. *Documents from Old Testament Times*. New York: Harper & Bros., 1961.

Unger, Merrill F. *Biblical Demonology*. Wheaton: Van Kampen Press, Inc., 1952.

——————. *Israel and the Aramaeans of Damascus.* London: James Clarke & Co., LTD., 1957.

Wright, G. E. *Biblical Archaeology.* Philadelphia: The Westminster Press, 1957.

Young, E. J. *My Servants the Prophets.* Grand Rapids: Wm. B. Eerdmans Publishing Co., 1955.

ARTICLES AND PERIODICALS

Aharoni, Yohanan. "Arad: Its Inscriptions and Temple," *The Biblical Archaeologist,* XXXI, 1 (Feb., 1968).
——————. "Hebrew Ostraca from Tel Arad," *Israel Exploration Journal,* XVI, 1 (1966).
Albright, W. F. "New Light on the Early History of Phoenician Colonization," *Bulletin of the American Schools of Oriental Research,* LXXXIII, 83 (Oct., 1941).

Davis, John J. "Tombs Tell Tales," *Brethren Missionary Herald,* XXXI, 10 (May, 1969).
Dever, William G. "The Water Systems at Hazor and Gezer," *The Biblical Archaeologist,* XXXII, 3 (1969).

Freedman, David N. "The Second Season at Ancient Ashdod," *The Biblical Archaeologist,* XXVI, 4 (Dec., 1963).

Glueck, Nelson. "Ezion-geber," *The Biblical Archaeologist,* XXVIII, 3 (Sept., 1965).

Heicksen, Martin H. "Tekoa: Excavations in 1968," *Grace Journal,* X, 2 (Spring, 1969).

Malamat, A. "Aspects of the Foreign Policies of David and Solomon," *Journal of Near Eastern Studies,* XXII, 1 (Jan., 1963).
——————. "The Kingdom of David and Solomon in its Contact with Egypt and Aram Nahariam," *The Biblical Archaeologist,* XXI, 4 (Dec., 1958).
Mendelson, I. "Samuel's Denunciation of Kingship in the Light of the Akkadian Documents from Ugarit," *Bulletin of the American Schools of Oriental Research,* No. 143 (Oct., 1956).

Pritchard, James B. "Industry and Trade at Biblical Gibeon," *The Biblical Archaeologist,* XXIII, 1 (Feb., 1960).

Sinclair, Lawrence A. "An Archaeological Study of Gibeah (Tell el-Ful)," *The Biblical Archaeologist*, XXVII, 2 (May, 1964).

Smith, James. "The Life and Thoughts of the Pre-Literary Prophets," *The Seminary Review*, XIII, 4 (Summer, 1967).

Ussishkin, D. "King Solomon's Palace and Building 1723 in Megiddo," *Israel Exploration Journel*, XVI, 3 (1966).

Wright, G. Ernest. "Fresh Evidence for the Philistine Story," *The Biblical Archaeologist*, XXIX, 3 (Sept., 1966).

——————. "Philistine Coffins and Mercenaries," *The Biblical Archaeologist*, XXII, 3 (Sept., 1959).

——————. "The Steven's Reconstruction of the Solomonic Temple," *The Biblical Archaeologist*, XVIII, 2 (May, 1955).

Yadin, Y. "Let the Young Men, I Pray Thee, Arise and Play Before Us," *Journal of the Palestine Oriental Society*, XXI (1948).

——————. "The Fifth Season of Excavations at Hazor," *The Biblical Archaeologist*, XXXII, 3 (1969).

NAME INDEX

SCRIPTURE INDEX